# DON'T SMOKE
## THE NEWSPAPER!
## And Other Lessons Learned
## by a Pastor

John P. King

ISBN-13: 978-0615662954

Cover design by T. James Kay

*Don't Smoke the Newspaper* is a delightful look at the life experiences of a young minister with a heart of gold. You will laugh, you may cry, but you will definitely be moved by the wit and wisdom of John P. King. I highly recommend *Don't Smoke the Newspaper* as a must read for those seeking God's hand in everyday life.

> Rev. Gene Markland – author *Spirit Fellowship, Experiencing Life in the Presence of God.*


This book is filled with rich and fulfilling life applications. It's rewarding for both young and old and great for Sunday School and Bible study.

> Angela Mays – author *God's Chosen Woman*


This book communicates on so many levels the heartfelt compassion that I him have come to expect from its author, John P. King. This volume will regale with laughter. It will cause the heart to pause and consider the wisdom of the message being delivered with each chapter, and challenge the heart with the penetrating questions John poses in each situation. In this volume the heart of a God given pastor comes through. To the wounded soul you will find comfort here.. I heartily recommend this book.

> Rev Michael Plemmons


*Don't Smoke the Newspaper* is a good read with many laughs. It is full of adventure and purpose.

> Carlos Garcia – author *I Choose You*

## DEDICATION

For my wife, Genevieve,
my kids, Kenneth and Emily,
and my parents, Buddy and Eileen,
who have lovingly and patiently
endured many years' worth of my "stupid stuff."

## ACKNOWLEDGEMENTS

A special thanks to my editor, Abigail Phillips, without whose help and encouragement this project would still probably be on the shelf.

Thank you to my first-round readers: Destry and Cami, Lisa, John, David, Mike, and Gene. I appreciate your comments and patience.

# CONTENTS

# INTRODUCTION

Everyone has their pet peeves and the things that make them crazy. If you ask my wife and kids what drives me nuts, they will tell you, "stupid stuff." Of course, I am not immune to doing stupid things. The evidence will be made abundantly clear as you read through this book. So just what is stupid stuff? The things that shouldn't happen and yet seem to abound just because someone didn't take the time to think through what they were about to do. Usually the end results are disastrous.

Stupid questions also fall into this category. Is there such a thing as a stupid question? You bet your life. We have all heard the axiom, "There is no such thing as a stupid question." I firmly believe that the stupid question exists. Some things don't need to be asked and shouldn't be asked. A good number of stupid questions start with, "What would happen if I . . ." Like, "What would happen if I stuck this into the electrical outlet?" If you have to ask, you probably don't want to know.  Some stupid questions are asked because the *asker* wasn't paying attention in the first place.  The math teacher says, "Do all of the even numbered problems for homework tonight."  The genius in the third row raises his hand and asks, "Do you want us to do the odd ones, too?"  Stupid stuff and stupid questions do not have to happen.

Stupid stuff includes the unexplained.  Bizarre things happen every day that defy explanation.  Everyone has experienced this.  You go through some unusual circumstances, and you can't quite make heads or tails out of what just happened—not that what has happened was bad—you just can't figure out the why's and the how's.  If you're like me, you like knowing what is going on.  An unsatisfied sense of curiosity makes my head spin.

This book is full of stupid stuff (with many more things left unwritten). In fact, every chapter has a "stupid" title.  Most of the stories fit the first definition of stupid stuff—those things that happened that shouldn't have.  There are also a few stories that defy explanation and simply leave you scratching your head.  Hopefully, you'll get a good laugh out of the things I have seen and done (yes, I have actually done quite a bit of the "stupid stuff"). However, here is the warning. DO NOT ATTEMPT THE THINGS WRITTEN HEREIN. I am not a professional and have survived only by the grace of God. I will not be held liable for your pain, suffering, injury, and humiliation for doing what you read here. The point is to learn the lessons attached to each chapter, not to repeat the obvious foolishness (with the exception of the last chapter—in that case, "fool away").

To that end, each chapter includes "Think About It" questions. These questions are designed to help you think through your own experiences in light of the truths presented. You can read and work through this book by yourself; however, I would highly recommend going through this book with another person. Being able to share your answers with someone else has a dynamic way of bringing deeper understanding, not only of yourself but also in what God has been and is doing in your life. There's also nothing like sharing your own stupid stories for the simple shock value of seeing the expression on your friend's face. This book is also ideal for Sunday School classes and small group settings because the questions are designed to foster dialogue.

I would love to hear from you! Feel free to contact me at my email address, smokingnewspaper@gmail.com. It would delight me to know that I am not the only stupid person on the planet who had to learn some things the hard way. My hope is that what I have experienced will, in some way, bring you closer to God. Believe it or not, it has done just that for me. I would love to hear about these kinds of stories most of all. So with no further delay, let the stupidity begin.

Joy in Christ,

John P. King

# CHAPTER ONE

## Stupid Influence
## or
## Don't Smoke the
## Newspaper

I grew up in the suburbs, but that doesn't mean there weren't opportunities to get into trouble and do amazingly stupid things. In the summer time, the neighborhood kids—probably about twenty of us—would stay out to all hours of the night. Opportunities for stupidity abounded.

My older brother, Alan, and I played with Steve and Mike more than any of the other kids on the block. They always had some off-the-wall story about their Uncle Alex. They thought a lot of their uncle, and it was easy to understand why. The few occasions I actually spent any time with him left me with the impression that this guy had it going on. Alex was strong, charismatic, jovial, and seemed to always know what he was talking about. However, Uncle Alex was also quite the instigator and constantly tried to get his nephews to do something outrageous, invariably getting them into trouble with their parents.

One day, when I was around nine years old, the four of us were outside playing when Steve piped up and said, "Guess what Uncle Alex told us?" Good old Uncle Alex had bestowed some of his knowledge concerning the fine art of smoking on his all-too-eager nephews. He told Steve that newspaper could be rolled up and smoked. So, we sent Steve home to get some newspaper and matches, and when he returned, we all proceeded to the grove of trees behind my house for cover.

Looking back now, what Uncle Alex probably said was that you could smoke newspaper; as in, tear off a little piece, roll it up, and tie a granny knot in the middle of it. However, Steve told us that you could smoke *a* newspaper. So Alan rolled up an *entire sheet* of newspaper and tied a simple granny knot in the middle of it, believing that we were following Uncle Alex's instructions. We stood in a circle, and as we prepared to light it, we all came to the decision that since it was Steve's uncle who had imparted such wisdom to us, it was only fair that Steve should get first crack at our homemade, world-class sized cigarette.

At our ages, none of us were seasoned smokers, but we knew enough by watching others what smoking should look like. Alan lit one end of the paper and blew out the flame. Much to our surprise, the lit end continued to glow red and smolder, just like a cigarette would. We thought that when the flame went out, that would be the end of it. Hmm, maybe Uncle Alex was right.

Steve took the paper, stuck it in his mouth, and proceeded to inhale . . . nothing. No smoking. He tried and tried and tried. Nothing but lots of **nothing**. The end smoldered and smoked, but Steve didn't get any of it for himself. Exasperated, Alan asked for a turn, and Steve handed it over with a great degree of disappointment over not having any success. Alan was determined to make this thing work. He put it in his mouth and kept taking breath after breath. It was deadly silent in those woods except for the rhythmic sound of my brother sucking wind in his vain attempt to smoke the paper.

I had had enough. With a "My turn," I snatched the "cigarette" out of Alan's hands. I was going to show these people how to do it. Undaunted by the somewhat-soggy cigarette, I put it in my mouth and drew, but there was nothing. I did it again and still had no success. This was not as easy as I'd hoped it would be. I exhaled as much as I could to prepare for another drag. I put every bit of strength my little lungs could muster into that the third pull. Halfway into my draw, the cigarette finally gave up its prize. Somewhere in the knot of the paper, something broke loose and smoke suddenly and violently filled my lungs.

I thought I was going to die. With a loud "PUUUUUUUUUHHHHHH," the biggest cloud of black, acrid smoke came pouring out of my face. It came out of my mouth and nose and it sure enough felt like it was coming out of my eyes and ears. I was "feeling the burn." I could hear everyone around me cheering, but I could only see two things—smoky blackness and stars. Alan patted me on the back and said with great excitement, "Do it again. Do it again! That was cool!"

My brain was swimming, my nose running, my head and chest felt like a screaming inferno, and I was having such a coughing fit, I believed that at any moment my lungs were going to come out of my mouth. The dizziness almost brought me to my knees. To top it off, the residual taste made me gag. I wanted NO PART of "Do it again!" My only goal was to pass off the uber-cigarette as fast as I could. Someone else needed to join me in my pain. Honestly, I cannot remember anything after the moment that Alan took the newspaper out of my hands. All I knew was that Uncle Alex was right: you can smoke a newspaper. I also knew I would *never* trust Uncle Alex again, and if Steve or Mike ever volunteered another of their uncle's pearls of wisdom, someone was going to get slapped.

But really, why should I be mad at their uncle? He didn't roll the newspaper. He didn't light it. He didn't "make" us smoke it. We did that all by ourselves. At the same time, we knew that what we were doing would not meet with our parents' approval. We certainly didn't ask permission, and we deliberately took shelter in the woods, away from prying eyes. So what brought on this particular adventure?

Influence.

Uncle Alex had influence over our lives. The mystique that surrounded him gave him sway over what we did. It impacted our decisions and behavior. We had heard enough lectures from our parents and teachers alike to know that smoking was beyond unhealthy. And yet, we allowed this one man's momentary, fleeting statement to override everything we had been taught—even to the point that it wasn't a cigarette or cigar that we attempted to smoke, but a NEWSPAPER. As bad as the things are that go into cigarettes, can you image the horrible ingredients in a newspaper? Just thinking about the ink alone makes me want to go back in time, snatch that little boy up and ask, "What are you doing?! Are you stupid?"

Yet, that is the power of influence. By default of their relationship with you, the people you surround yourself with as well as those you look up to hold a place of influence in your life. It is impossible to avoid. The things they say and do impact the way you think and behave. Steve and Mike had just as much influence on me as I had on them. Uncle Alex was someone I only saw a handful of times, but I allowed my perception of him to dictate my actions. I admired the man and wanted to be like him, so I did something he suggested. I did something I felt he would want me to do.

Influence also lies underneath the power of advertising. A celebrity becomes the "pitch man" for a product, solely because the ad agency knows that people want to be like those superstars. Peyton Manning endorses Wheaties. Michael Jordan wears Hanes underwear. Halle Berry is one of the faces of Revlon. Jamie Lee Curtis eats Activia yogurt. Who has ever spent any amount of significant time with these "heroes?" Yet we spend our money based on what they endorse. If we aren't careful about *who* influences us and *how*, we will end up becoming mere copies of someone else and do stupid things we ultimately end up regretting rather than being the person God wants us to be.

The Bible points this principle out in the book of Proverbs: "Do not make friends with a hot-tempered man, do not associate with one easily angered, or you may learn his ways and get yourself ensnared."[1] If we hang around an angry person, we end up becoming angry ourselves. The angry person doesn't end up becoming more self-controlled—we end up losing our control. I find it interesting that the downward pull of influence always exerts greater strength than the upward.  The apostle Paul said it this way: "Do not be deceived: bad company corrupts good morals."[2]

No one lives in a social vacuum.  God has made us social beings.  Yes, some people are more social than others, but the principle remains the same for everyone. Modern technology has even made leaving our houses irrelevant when it comes to influence.  On any given day, email, IM, Facebook, Twitter, Myspace, and webcams make it possible to influence and be influenced in countless ways.

We can be slaves to others' influences, or we can become the people God wants us to be through healthy influences.  We can change for the better.  We can find full expressions of life through interactions with others. We just have to be careful about where our influences emerge.  This demands purpose and intentionality from each of us.  Another proverb says, "He who walks with the wise will be wise, but the companion of fools will suffer harm."[3]

We need to allow people who are "better" than us to speak into our lives.  By "better" I mean those around us whose walk with the Lord is plainly evident and stronger than ours.  We need to observe them, learn from them, do what they do, spend time with them, and be accountable to them. This is something we have to go out of our way to do—it doesn't happen naturally. We all have a tendency to do what is easiest. The challenge to become more than what we are doesn't occur easily or expediently. Most of the time, it isn't any fun either. But in the end, it is always worth it!

That doesn't mean there won't be "fools" in our lives—they will always be there. We just shouldn't make them our close companions or be influenced by them. *We* can exert the influence. We should endeavor to impact others for the better. Speak to them the wisdom I would speak to you now: PUT THE NEWSPAPER DOWN!

## Think About It

- Who are the people from your past that have influenced you (both positively and negatively)?
- What things did you do because of their influence?
- What things do you do *now* because of their influence?

- Name five people in your life today that influence you.
- How are they influencing you for better or for worse?
- Who are you influencing?
- What are you doing to influence them, and what kind of impact are you having?

# CHAPTER TWO

# Stupidity Multiplied
# or
# A Case of the Martian
# Measles

The weird thing about getting into trouble is that it always seems to lead to a greater degree of trouble. At least, that's what I have found to be true. If we don't deal with "problems" immediately, they have a way of multiplying into circumstances that, in the end, are significantly worse than the original offense. Let me give you an example.

My older brother, Alan, and I had been sent to our rooms for some sort of misdeed, *again*. I cannot remember what it was that earned us our time out because what happened later landed us in so much more trouble that the initial issue eludes me. The only thing I can recall is the end of the matter.

My brother's room was across the hall from mine, and even though we had been given strict instructions to go to our own rooms and close the doors, well, that just wasn't going to last. Alan was ten, and I was six. Boredom comes quickly to little boys. Before long, we started talking under the cracks of our doors, then eventually cracking our doors open, then opening the doors, to finally talking openly across the hall. As you may have guessed, talking wasn't enough, and after a while, we needed more to entertain ourselves.

I don't know who fired the first shot, but one of us found a rubber band and hit the other one. I do remember tearing my room apart looking for as many rubber bands as I could find while Alan did the same. Between the two of us, we came up with about a dozen. We tried to be as quiet as we could, but two boys at war can raise quite a ruckus: we ran and jumped around in our rooms while slamming the doors to keep from getting shot, laughing and shouting through it all.

My mother yelled up the stairs at us, asking what it was that we were doing.  We yelled back the obvious answer: "Nothing!"  Being a parent myself, I have discovered that whenever my children answer any of my questions with "nothing," I had better investigate further.  On this occasion, my mom simply reiterated the present circumstances of our confinement from the bottom of the stairs—we were supposed to be in our own rooms with the doors closed.  She did not bother coming to enforce the punishment.

We IMMEDIATELY began carrying on, only trying to be quieter about it.  All of the rubber bands eventually broke, as they are prone to do, but our blood was up, and we set about looking for something else to use for ammunition.  We stumbled across a Cool Whip container full of split peas that Alan had used for a Cub Scout project.  There had to be hundreds of them.  Inspiration hit.  In digging through our toys and games, we also found a couple of straw-sized tubes.  Jackpot!

We divided the peas in half and then went to our respective rooms to carry on the conflict.  A Cool Whip container may not sound like much, but next time you have the chance, fill one up with some split peas, and feel free to dump it out on the floor.  It makes a surprisingly large mess. Now imagine two boys shooting them at each other like spit balls from room to room across a hallway. It is mess multiplied.

Loading the tube and shooting them one at a time became real tedious after about the fiftieth time. We discovered that if we put six or so in a straw, we could get a shotgun effect (too many more than that and the straw had a tendency to get clogged). However, even better than that was stuffing a bunch of them in our cheeks. We used our tongues to load the straws and fire them like machine guns. It's amazing what one will do for fun. I hate peas, and yet here I was with my mouth full of them all for the sake of lifting the boredom of my punishment.

With our new-found modes of combat, we quickly depleted our stockpiles of ammunition. So we did what any good little boys would do—we recycled. Our recycling had one unforeseen yet delightful consequence. The peas began to get a little soggy, which meant now they began to stick instead of merely bounce off. We took off our clothes and put on a pair of shorts so we could tell when one of us got hit as the peas were beginning to adhere to our skin. It wasn't long before we were both covered with little green pea-sized dots. We looked like we had a case of the Martian Measles.

As you may have guessed, the peas didn't just stick to us. They stuck to everything. They were on the hallway walls. They were on our bedroom doors. They were on the walls of our rooms. They were on our furniture. And the ones that weren't stuck to anything were, quite literally, everywhere else. We knew we were being noisy, so Alan came into my room, and we closed the door so as not to be found out. But it wasn't enough. We were still too loud.

Mom flung open my door as only a mom can do. BUSTED! And now came the aforementioned "end of the matter," which truly began with our "ends." She spanked us soundly and sent us straight to the shower. It was the longest shower any ten and six-year-old boys ever took—we didn't want to get out and face the remainder of our punishment.

When we did get out, a variety of cleaning supplies awaited us. Our task was to scrub the walls and furniture and to vacuum the floors of our rooms and the hallway. There would be no TV or going outside for the next week (one week doesn't sound like much now, but it's an eternity for a six year old). We would be confined to our rooms from the moment we got home from school except for the variety of jobs and chores we would be given in addition to our current daily list. We were sent to bed as soon as we finished cleaning up as many peas as we could find. Even with all the cleaning we did that night, we were still finding peas weeks later.

Like I said, unless there is some kind of intervention, trouble tends to lead to more trouble. A great example of this is found in the story of David and Bathsheba. As the prophet, Samuel, tells the story, we find David on the rooftop patio of his palace while his armies are besieging the Ammonite city of Rabbah.[1] In the city below, he sees Bathsheba taking a bath. David lingers. Mistake number one. Instead of turning away, lust begins to creep into his heart over this very attractive young lady. David had an eye for the ladies, and Bathsheba caught his full attention.

As king, David could marry any eligible woman he wanted, so he sets out to inquire who this lovely young lady is. Not only is she married, but she is also the wife of Uriah, a member of David's Special Forces. All of this should have ended there, but David sends messengers to bring her to the palace with really only one purpose in mind—to have sex with her. Mistake number two.

Lo and behold, Bathsheba gets pregnant. Imagine that. As if it wasn't a possibility. David now concocts a plan in order to cover up this potential scandal. Mistake number three. He sends for Uriah under the premise that he needs a report on the siege. The hope was that when Uriah came home from the war, he would behave like any man who hasn't seen the wife he loves for some time. Uriah should have come home with one thing on his mind: "Where's my woman?!" If Uriah slept with Bathsheba, it would deflect any question over an adulterous relationship because the baby would be assumed to be his. Things don't work out that simply. Uriah proved to have greater integrity than the king: he refused to be intimate with his wife while Israel and Judah camped in the open field with the Ark of the Covenant.

Desperation leads to a new phase of the plan. David deliberately gets Uriah drunk. He hoped that with his mind clouded by the effects of the alcohol, Uriah would "forget" his personal convictions and go home to his wife. The king attempted to undermine the integrity of his loyal and righteous subject, Uriah, by getting him to act against his conscience. Mistake number four. Uriah the Hittite may have been a foreigner, but he loved the Lord and refused to take comfort when the Ark of the Covenant was in danger, and the armies of Israel were in battle.

David could have stopped all of this foolishness at any time, but as the story is told, it leads to conspiracy and murder—mistakes five, six, seven, eight … David enlists Joab, one of his generals, in a plot to murder Uriah by using the war as a plausible reason for his death. In following the king's orders, Joab set up Uriah by placing him in the hottest part of the battle, the kind of place one of David's mighty men would want to be. Yet, at just the right moment, the Israeli forces were to withdraw, leaving Uriah on his own without support. Unfortunately, *this* part of the plan worked perfectly. Uriah gets an honorable death in battle and David gets Bathsheba, with no one being the wiser (those in the palace and army that knew of the events excluded, of course).

No one, that is, except for God. He knew what was going on, and through the prophet, Nathan, He laid David's egregious sins bare. This sordid affair reveals how circumstances can spiral out of control. It is so

John P. King

important to recognize bad decisions and bad behavior before they become an entity in themselves. Look at all the people who were hurt and dragged into this true-to-life soap opera as co-conspirators. It is a brave thing to challenge the king, but I have to ask, why did no one stand up for what was right and tell David that his conduct was shameful?

The answer may lie near the end of II Samuel. This section is an addendum to the book and should not be viewed in chronological order with the other events. It tells a series of unrelated stories that transpired during David's reign. In one of the stories, we see a time when Israel was engaged in battle with the Philistines.[2] During the battle, David became fatigued and an enemy combatant by the name of Ishbi-benob saw this. Ishbi deliberately targeted the king and came after him in his worn-out state. However, Abishai, another mighty man from David's Special Forces, intervened and saved David's life. At this point, David's men swore that he would never again see battle "so that you do not extinguish the lamp of Israel."[3] David willingly complied with their wishes even though they did not have the right or grounds to make such a request. No one stood up to David's scandalous behavior with

Bathsheba because he was exactly where they wanted him to be—at home. Therefore, when David's army waged war against the Ammonites, David was on the palace rooftop, ogling the local babes.

The kingdom of God does not work the way the world does. Leaders are supposed to lead, not take places of comfort and ease. Even if David did not engage in combat, he should have at least camped out with his troops in the field. His God-appointed place was to be with his men. The anointed king belongs at the head of his army. Instead of doing the work he was called to do, David was enjoying the "benefits of kingship." He traded in his responsibilities for the good life.

This leads to a point that I cannot stress enough. Although the story of David and Bathsheba is filled with misdeed after misdeed, this whole ordeal happened because David wasn't doing something he should have been doing. Often the trouble we find ourselves in is not a matter of *doing* something we *shouldn't*; rather, it is a matter of *not doing* something we *should*.

The Christian life is sometimes perceived as a list of rules concerning things we aren't supposed to do along with the "fun stuff" we have to give up in order to follow Christ. Jesus didn't give his life for us so that we could not do things. He has appointed us and anointed us to live out a plan full of purpose. As the Lord said through the prophet Jeremiah, "'For I know the plans I have for you,' declares the Lord, 'plans to prosper you and not to harm you, plans to give you hope and a future.'"[4] The apostle Paul put it this way: "For we are His workmanship, created in Christ Jesus for good works, which God prepared beforehand so that we would walk in them."[5] If we focus on the things that God has given us to do, there won't be time to even consider doing things we shouldn't.

Pastors, priests, and ministers are not the only people who have a specific calling. God has given everyone talents and gifts. He has created a plan and given each of us an anointing to do something. I believe our greatest times of trouble begin when we aren't following that plan and doing what we have been anointed to do. We have cashed in our responsibilities for something easier and more enjoyable, as King David did. President Theodore Roosevelt once said, "Never throughout history has a man who lived a life of ease left a name worth remembering."[6]

Want to stay out of trouble and avoid a case of the Martian Measles? Then follow the great plan of purpose that God has for your life.

## Think About It

- We all have weaknesses (remember: David's was women). What are your weaknesses and the things that have the potential to lead you into trouble?
- How difficult is it for you to recognize when you are starting down a path of trouble?
- What kinds of changes in your life need to be made so that when you get into trouble, you deal with it right away without it getting worse?
- Who are the people in your life that help keep you accountable when you get into trouble?

# CHAPTER THREE

## Stupidity's Reward
## or
## The Stupid Shall Be Punished

My first senior pastorate was a small church in the town of Princess Anne, Maryland. I had to work an additional job in order to provide for my family because the church was very small. Without a doubt, I enjoyed this job more than any other non-ministerial position I have ever had. I worked as the Juvenile Clerk (irony of ironies, considering the next chapter) for the Clerk of the Circuit Court of Somerset County.

Every job has things about it that are enjoyable and things that are a drag. Along with looking after the juvenile case files, which was interesting, I also had to help out with the land records as they came into the courthouse. I hated doing the land records. Look up *boring* or *tedious* in the dictionary, and you will see a picture of some sap documenting, cataloging, and filing all manner of land records. However, my favorite part of the job was sitting in the courtroom at the clerk's bench, taking notes on the trial proceedings. I noted major points of the trial: the people present, the various motions, the evidence given, and the swearing in of witnesses.

Others in the clerk's office also sat at the bench, but they didn't like manning the desk. Since I loved every minute of it, I would ask them if I could take their posts, and they were always willing to oblige. People's lives played out in that courtroom. It beat any show on TV. Sometimes the cases were funny, sometimes tragic, and sometimes they made me angry. It was real people with real consequences, and I never found it boring.

Once a month we had Violation of Probation day. On this particular day, we had all of those people in the court that, for some reason or another, had violated the terms of their probation from a previous conviction. This day tended to be like a circus. A pile of cases always awaited us, and as such, we tried to get through them as quickly as possible; otherwise, we could be there well into late afternoon.

Everyone who received probation had standard conditions they had to meet, like paying court costs and visiting their probation officer. Depending on the kind of crime they committed, they might have to meet special conditions, like submitting to urinalysis tests, avoiding contact with certain people, and having to abide by a curfew.

We had one absolutely unforgettable gentleman make his way through our court. His original charges were drug related, so part of his special conditions included submitting to urine tests to make sure he wasn't taking drugs. All through his case, he kept pointing to the fact that he had not had a "hot UA." All of his scheduled and random court-ordered urinalysis tests had come back negative for any kind of drugs. He also talked about how he had met all the terms of his probation, including all the appointments with his probation officer. I'll never forget the way he kept saying over and over, "Your honor, I ain't had a hot UA. I'm not taking no drugs."

Drug usage was not the issue. You found yourself in court on VOP day because you had violated *something*, and this guy had done the one thing for which this judge had no tolerance: not paying court costs. Judge Long was a great judge, and I really admired him. From what I saw, he applied the law fairly to everyone that came to his court and rendered just decisions. Although he was a stickler on court costs, he went to great lengths to accommodate those who had to pay them by making a payment schedule that the individual could realistically meet.

This "probation violator" had actually stopped paying. He had been abiding by the terms of payment for quite a while, but at some point, he simply quit paying what had been ordered by the court. The judge kept asking him why he hadn't fulfilled what he was ordered to pay. The man danced around the question, never answering it directly.

He'd done all of the hard stuff his probation agreement had required, including staying clean, yet he hadn't done the easiest thing, which was to pay the costs and fees associated with his trial. If I remember correctly, he had been ordered to pay $5 a week. No amount of explaining or pleading was going to help him. The judge rendered that he had violated his probation, and subsequently ordered the man taken into custody immediately to serve out the remainder of his original sentence. The sad part was that this guy was near the end of his probation—another week or so and he would have been completely free.

Talk about stupid. For the cost of a meal at McDonald's, this fellow ended up in jail. The stupid shall be punished. That, however, is not the end of the story. After court ended for the day and I was packing up the files, one of the sheriff's deputies who had placed the man in the holding cell came bouncing back into the courtroom and said to me, "Guess what just happened!"

Are you kidding me? How was I supposed to know what just happened? I wasn't in the mood for a game of twenty questions, considering all of the follow-up work that had to be completed. The jumpy and anxious way he approached the desk fairly annoyed me as well. So I let him talk on without really paying much attention to him.

However, he got all of my attention when he explained the reason for his excitement. Our good buddy who had not failed a single drug test during his probationary period just failed a drug test of another kind. Every time someone is taken into custody and placed in one of the courthouse holding cells, the person has to be searched. Would you believe this guy came to court with a variety of controlled substances on him? When the deputies performed their routine search, they found a veritable cornucopia of drugs.

You could have knocked me over with a feather. This guy had some nerve. He stood before the judge begging for leniency based on his clean test record, and all the while his pockets were stuffed with all kinds of contraband. Did he expect to be let off probation? Was he preparing for some kind of after-court liberation party? It's impossible to say. The deputy warned me not to tell Judge Long. If he found out about it ahead of time, he would have to recuse himself from hearing the case, and he would want to hear this one.

When Drug Boy's hearing came up, the judge was absolutely incensed at this guy's audacity. The stupid was punished. The judge threw everything he could at him, and the perpetrator responded with indignation of his own.

Really? Ultimately, who was to blame? There's no point in getting angry at the judge, the cops, or anyone else for that matter. No one put those drugs in his pockets or made him carry them. Getting new charges and more jail time was no one else's fault but his, and I bet you would agree. And yet, when we get what *we* deserve, isn't that usually the first thing we do? Don't we look for someone else to blame?

Scripture contains all kinds of warnings about the consequences of sin. The apostle Paul wrote, "Do not be deceived, God is not mocked; for whatever a man sows, this he will also reap. For the one who sows to his own flesh will from the flesh reap corruption, but the one who sows to the Spirit will from the Spirit reap eternal life. Let us not lose heart in doing good, for in due time we will reap if we do not grow weary."[1]

It isn't that God is looking for people to squash. He doesn't delight in acting as the great hammer in the sky just waiting for us to get out of line so He can crack us one. It's just a fundamental law of existence. We reap what we sow. Apple trees make apples. Tomato plants grow tomatoes. If we indulge ourselves in the whims and desires of the selfish, sinful nature, we will reap its corruption and appropriate punishments. If we indulge ourselves in God's Spirit and Word, then we will reap the good plan He has for our lives. This includes eternal life and rewards that cannot be imagined.

We should also take note of God's underlying motive in punishment. The author of Hebrews put it this way: "My son, do not make light of the Lord's discipline, and do not lose heart when he rebukes you, because the Lord disciplines those he loves, and he punishes everyone he accepts as a son."[2] God will correct those He loves to help them become better people; however, it isn't punishment for punishment's sake. The passage goes on: ". . . but God disciplines us for our good, so that we may share in His holiness. No discipline seems pleasant at the time, but painful. Later on, however, it produces a harvest of righteousness and peace for those who have been trained by it."[3]

So the whole point of God's discipline is not just to change our behavior but to allow us to share in His holiness and righteousness. Should we be surprised, then, that God corrects us when we get out of line? Every government on the planet has its list of laws and the punishments that go with them. Let me ask you—when was the last time you got something from your governmental authorities for following the law? I'd say likely never. Cops don't pull people over for driving the speed limit in order to give them a prize. They pull them over for speeding and give them a ticket with a nice fat fine. If you don't like receiving consequences, then don't do things that you know are wrong. If you don't like paying speeding tickets and want to keep your driver's license, then quit speeding. If you don't like getting spanked by God, then quit breaking His commandments, laws, and precepts, and start living in the righteousness and peace that come through His training.

In Deuteronomy, God presented the Israelites with all of the blessings that follow obedience along with the consequences for disobedience.[4] *Unlike* human government, God gives out all kinds of rewards and blessings for obedience. But *like* human government, He punishes the disobedient. God would much prefer to give good things to you. When the Israelites accepted the terms of God's covenantal relationship, the Lord went on to say, "I call heaven and earth to witness against you today, that I have set before you life and death, the blessing and the curse. So choose life in order that you may live, you and your descendants, by loving the Lord our God, by obeying His voice, and by holding fast to Him."[5]

However, even with the disposition to reward, He will absolutely dispense judgment and consequences without reservation or hesitation to those who defy Him through disobedience. We have all received a fair warning. There is no point in getting mad at anyone but ourselves if we get what we deserve for being bad. As Forrest Gump would say, "Stupid is as stupid does." The stupid shall be punished.

## Think About It

- When have you received exactly what you deserved for being bad? Who did you blame for your consequences? Are you *still* mad about it?
- What lesson did you learn?

# CHAPTER FOUR

## Stupid Mercy

## or

## Shooting Cars Is a Bad Idea

Among the stupid things I have done, this story marks as the crowning achievement. In fact, this particular event is so beyond the pale that until the writing of this book, my parents had no idea that I had done such a thing. Here at the age of 42, I am still afraid of what may happen when they find out.

The family that lived next door had three kids: Sharon, Jay, and Mike. After being our neighbors for six years, they were moving away. My brother, sister, and I had been good friends with them, although there were plenty of occasions where our association was less than beneficial.

I was around thirteen at the time, and I had the chance to spend the night at Mike's house as a sort of last hurrah before he moved. Initially, Steve, of newspaper-smoking fame, hung out with us. Boys being boys, we became bored fairly quickly since most of Mike's belongings were packed in preparation for the move. It dawned on the three of us that it would be a lot of fun if we unpacked the BB guns and shot cars as they drove by. My parents wouldn't let me have a BB gun and, unbeknownst to them, I had bought one from another boy in the neighborhood for fifteen dollars. Considering the evening's entertainment we had devised, is it any wonder why? Mike kept my gun at his house so that my parents wouldn't find out, but now he was moving away. There was no way I could keep my gun hidden from my parents if I brought it home. So I'd consigned myself to the reality that it had to go with Mike when he moved. Before that happened, there would be one last adventure with my gun. Steve went home to get his, and the three of us snuck out after dark.

Our homes were on a cul-de-sac in the middle of a larger block of houses. We took our positions under some bushes a few houses away, near the top of the street.  Looking back on this little escapade, I can't help thinking why we didn't set up somewhere else in the neighborhood much further away from our homes.  But, this chapter isn't called smart mercy, it's called stupid mercy, and boy, were we being stupid.

Since we lived in the back of our neighborhood, the road around our block was not exactly the busiest.  So, a car came by about every ten minutes, and when it did, one of us would load up and shoot it.  Yes, that's right—we shot the cars as they drove by.  During the down time between cars, we would shoot the mailboxes along the street and whatever else caught our eye.  Shooting any glass or windows was a no-no because we knew that might "get us into trouble."

Steve's parents wanted him home by 10:00, so when the time came, he left.  Mike and I kept up the fun, but as the saying goes, "All good things must come to an end."  Our end came about ten minutes later with screeching tires and a lot of yelling.  I don't remember who shot the car, but the driver was obviously no one to be trifled with.  Before the hollow THUMP of the BB sound had faded, the car made an immediate hard left and turned down my street, followed by screeching tires as the car came to an abrupt halt. The owner of the pinged vehicle stood in the middle of our street and hollered at the top of his voice, "COME OUT OF YOUR HOUSES!"

Mike and I KNEW the gig was up the moment that car made its agile turn. The worst panic I have ever felt in my life gripped my very soul. When that man began to yell, a burst of adrenaline hit me like a bolt of lightning. Given the "fight or flight" reactionary options we each encounter, believe me—it was flight that ruled. To this day, I don't remember which way Mike went— he literally seemed to vanish into thin air. My adolescent legs took me as fast as they could away from the offended party, which happened to be the *long* way around the block. I ran through hedgerows, jumped over fences, and cut through backyards while tripping, stumbling, falling, scrambling, and trying to find a way back home without getting caught. Eventually I found myself in Mike's backyard. Given my long route, it was no surprise that Mike was already there. I was scraped up, scratched up, and out of breath, all the while trying to come up with some kind of workable plan to get back in the house with no one being the wiser.

Fortunately, Mike's parents had some visitors over that evening, and they were leaving just as Mike and I snuck in the house. It made for great cover as the whole family stood at the front door saying good-bye. We left the guns in the backyard and crept in through the garage. It was scary, but after taking off our shoes and crouching as low as we could, we managed to make it down the hall to his room without being noticed. His bedroom door had been closed and the light off during our adventure so it was possible to play it off like we had been sleeping.

We proceeded to strip down to our underwear and give our hair and eyes a good rubbing to make it appear that we had already gone to bed. As the front door shut, we came out of his room, saying we were sorry we'd missed saying good-bye to the visitors, and then asked what all that commotion was outside with the yelling and screaming. His parents laughed at our appearance and told us to go back to bed. Our ruse seemed to have worked.

Just when we were beginning to feel a little better, a new thought occurred to us—what if the driver came back the next day? A new phase of the plan had to be thought out, and it started with convincing Mike's parents to let us sleep in the basement. We knew we needed to retrieve the rifles from the backyard, and the best way to do this would be if we could spend the night downstairs, giving us access to the back door. Mike's mom and dad gave us the green light, and we proceeded to move all our pillows and blankets to our new "sleeping" area.

The moment we got to the basement, we quietly went out the back door and retrieved the BB guns. You have never seen two rifles get emptied, wrapped in newspaper, and buried amongst other packed materials so fast in all your life. And when I say buried, I mean BURIED. We found the biggest pile of boxes and bags and put them on the very bottom. It was a serious task, considering the rest of the house had gone to bed at this point, and every little sound we made felt like it was reverberating off the walls. We expected Mike's mom or dad to come downstairs at any moment to investigate the racket we made as we moved mounds of packed household goods in our vain attempt to assuage our fear.

With the task of hiding the evidence behind us, we tried to go to sleep, but the silence was more than I could take. The only thing I could hear was that man

yelling over and over, "COME OUT OF YOUR HOUSES!"
Mike was in the same sorry state. It was as if we were
still outside under those bushes. High anxiety was the
mood of the night. Up to that point, nothing we had
done to abate our fear had worked. We knew that when
morning came, it would bring our certain doom. Our
hope lay in one final, desperate option . . . PRAY!

Although Mike was Catholic and I was United
Methodist, we had no interfaith animosity that night.
Differences in theology went out the window as we
united in prayer, begging God to bail us out. We were in
complete harmony and agreement as we languished
before the Lord, promising Him everything and
anything if He would rescue us from our impending
demise. It was my first all-night prayer meeting.

I packed my things in the morning and went
home before Mike's or my parents woke up. The only
refuge was my bedroom, and I went straight there. My
bed felt like a safe place, so I laid down and tried to
sleep, but I kept waking up over and over with the
overwhelming need to look out the window to see if *he*
was coming. And miracle of miracles, each time I looked
out, he wasn't there.

Later that afternoon, I finally summoned up the courage to go outside and talk to Steve and Mike about the previous night's fiasco. Steve informed us that the driver actually came up to his house and started banging on the front door, demanding they come out. Thankfully, Steve's dad slammed the door on the guy, after which he drove away. And here the three of us stood, waiting for him to come back. He didn't. Not that day or the next.

The following Saturday, I helped Mike's family move, and still we hadn't seen the man. To our shock, and cautious glee, he never returned. When I take time to think about what could have happened if we had been found out, I shudder. Let's face it. What we did is the kind of thing that gets people a free ride in the back of a police car, complete with a set of shiny bracelets. We could have ended up in juvenile hall. As it was, we actually got away with it. There were absolutely *no* repercussions for our act of blatant vandalism. Well, at least none beyond having to live through the terror of the experience.

Jesus told a parable called The Lost Son, but it is better known as The Prodigal Son.[1] Even though this is a well-known story, the word *prodigal* doesn't mean what most people think it means. Most teaching on this parable implies that *prodigal* carries the idea of being lost or wayward, but the word actually means "recklessly wasteful; extravagant." It is from the Latin word, *prodigere*, which means, "to squander."[2] That is exactly what the prodigal son did with his inheritance: he squandered it.

You know this guy has some nerve when he approaches his father and asks for the inheritance that will one day be his as a son. Dear old dad lives and breathes and yet, the son wants what is coming to him now. Wow! A story that starts out this way can only go from bad to worse. The boy spends all his money, his inheritance, *prodigiously*. If there is a party, he is there. If there isn't a party, he's going to start one. Should we be surprised when he becomes destitute? We eventually find him serving a foreigner by feeding his pigs. The kid reaches such a low point that he ends up eating the same slop he served to the pigs.

When the son realizes just how good he had it at home, he makes a decision to return, but not for the position he had when he left. He knows what he has done is unforgivable, so he plans to offer himself as a servant to his father. Here we see his heart: "Father I have sinned against heaven, and in your sight; I am no longer worthy to be called your son; make me as one of your hired men."[3]

Now comes the part we all love. The father, never having given up hope for his son, waits with great expectation for his return, having spent countless days and hours watching the road in hope that "today" might be the day. Today finally comes. The father runs to his boy, embraces, and kisses him. The father will have none of this foolish talk of being a servant. His son has returned. He tells his servants, "Dress him in the finest. Kill the fatted calf. Tonight there will be a feast. All is forgiven."

Such is the great mercy of God. He always forgives, and sometimes, we get away with it— whatever "it" is. I know this is rather puzzling, considering the topic of the last chapter (The Stupid Shall Be Punished), but we are talking about God. As made evident by this parable, sometimes God exercises His prerogative to let the whole of a matter go, just like He did for Mike and me. His mercy and love are that big.

For those who know the parable, you know that it has more to say. The older brother finds out what's going on, and he is so angry, he won't even go inside his father's house. In fact, the older brother might have been saying, "COME OUT OF THE HOUSE!" His irresponsible sibling, who spent everything on wild living, has come home and received a hero's welcome. Dad has to come out and express why this is such a momentous day: "for this brother of yours was dead and has begun to live, and was lost and has been found."[4]

Actually, this second half of the parable contains the greater point. The Prodigal Son is the third in a series of parables along with the Lost Sheep and the Lost Coin. Jesus addressed these parables to the Pharisees and teachers of the law to highlight their terrible attitude. They were incensed because Jesus spent a considerable amount of time with tax collectors and sinners. The rabble of society dined with Jesus while the Pharisees and scribes stood by in a seemingly secondary position. Or were they?

As the father said to the older brother, "Son, you have always been with me, and all that is mine is yours. But we had to celebrate and rejoice . . ."[5] In the same way, the religious leadership, the Pharisees and scribes, were in a position to know God better than the rest of society. Yet, when the mercy of God was demonstrated before their very eyes, instead of rejoicing, they became indignant. Isn't that what we do as well? In reflecting on my little adventure, you may have asked, "What about the poor sap that was driving the car?" Letting the matter go for Mike and me seems seriously unfair to the man who owned the car we shot.

Without justice, a society will fall apart, but why do we always look for justice first instead of mercy? We all want justice . . . until it's our turn. Then, all of a sudden, we are looking for leniency, forgiveness, and a second chance. We look for mercy. When we see a person get away with some kind of misdeed, big or small, perhaps instead of looking for someone to blame, we should be looking for the hand of God. The Lord may be doing a work in them that we are totally unaware of and ultimately may never know this side of heaven (wait until chapter seven).

Two passages in Scripture beautifully carry this thought. First, the apostle Paul writes about judging others and concludes with the need for us to recognize the fact that one day we will all stand before God.[6] In the middle of the passage, we find this wondrous verse: "Or do you think lightly of the riches of His kindness and tolerance and patience, not knowing that the kindness of God leads you to repentance?"[7]

The second passage relates to when St. Peter talks about the coming day when Jesus will return. He encourages us to not give up on waiting for Jesus' return. It feels like the second coming of Christ may never happen. Why is Jesus taking so long? Peter reveals why: "The Lord is not slow in keeping His promise, as some understand slowness. He is patient with you, not wanting for anyone to perish, but everyone to come to repentance."[8]

God is looking to be kind and patient because that is what draws and keeps people, including you. Do you want God's kindness or His wrath? Do you want His patience or His anger? Do you want His mercy or His judgment? King David knew what he wanted. In both Psalm 6 and 38, he asked God not to discipline him in His anger. Can we not give God the freedom to do for others what we would want Him to do for us? We have a kind Father waiting at the end of the road ready to forgive, and there's always going to be an angry brother yelling, "COME OUT OF YOUR HOUSES!" Which will you give: mercy, or judgment? Who will you be: the father, or the older brother?

## Think About It

- How has God been kind to you? What have you "gotten away with"?

- How did that make you feel?

- What have others "gotten away with" during your lifetime?

- How did that make you feel?

- Have you ever had the opportunity to give someone mercy, kindness, and forgiveness, and let him or her "get away with" something?

- How did that make you feel?

# CHAPTER FIVE

## Stupid Love

## or

## The Free Pepsi Dance

Fourth of July weekend was going to be a fun one for our family. My wife and daughter were heading to the mountains, and my son, Kenneth, (eleven at the time) and I had a variety of "manly" activities laid out for the weekend. With the rigors of church and ministry, it had been a while since we had been able to have some mommy-daughter and father-son time, so we were really looking forward to the planned events.

On Saturday, after a day of outdoor, guy-oriented fun, Kenneth and I prepared to cap it off with some indoor activities. We had picked up a couple of frozen pizzas, highly caffeinated sodas, and some ice cream. The plan was to gorge ourselves into the wee hours of the morning while watching TV and playing one of our favorite games, *Axis & Allies*, A&A. This board game is intense. It takes a good fifteen minutes just to set up the board and sometimes days to finish one game. We were ready to be up all night.

A baseball game and a NASCAR race were on at the same time, so we happily bounced back and forth between the two. This would have driven my wife nuts. She would rather have to endure a show she can't stand than have to put up with what she calls "blip-o-vision;" constant changing of the channels. But she wasn't home. It was MAN night and we would watch however many channels at one time that we wanted.

Having said all of that, I have to note that as the evening went on, the race proved to be more exciting than the baseball game. The time came when they ran an obviously pre-recorded commercial featuring Jeff Gordon. He said that if he won the race, everyone in the country would get a free 2-liter bottle of a new product called Pepsi Edge. It should also be noted that the race was the Pepsi 400 in Daytona. One of Jeff's sponsors was Pepsi, so the car he was driving had a special Pepsi paint scheme, unlike his normal DuPont paint job. Fate seemed to be converging. For that reason, we ended up watching more of the race than the game, especially when it came to the final third.

Jeff had been running a good race and was proving to be a contender. Kenneth and I became enraptured in the prospect of our free soda and our game of A&A began to go unnoticed. There were 160 laps in the race, and Jeff was leading for the fourth time during laps 113-137. He lost the lead to Dale Earnhardt, Jr. on lap 138, but we didn't lose hope because Jeff had a great car that night, and he was driving it well.

It was a furious race. Before the end, there would be five more lead changes in those short 22 laps. Tony Stewart took over the lead on lap 142, and it seemed he might take it to the finish line. Jeff was right there, and Kenneth and I could hardly contain our excitement. Could Jeff pull it off? Could Tony keep him at bay? Would we get our free drink?

It seemed impossible, but Jeff finally overtook Tony on lap 154, only six laps from the finish. We began to believe! Nothing could take our attention from the TV. We were spellbound. In our excitement, we turned the volume up so high it sounded like the cars were in the room with us. Five laps. Four laps. Three laps. He was doing it. Jeff was doing it! Two laps. LAST LAP! We were on our feet, screaming and yelling. FINISH LINE! JEFF GORDON WINS! FREE PEPSI FOR ALL!

We jumped on the furniture, we hugged, laughed, yelled, and when there was no other way to express our delight, we created . . . the FREE PESPSI DANCE! It is hard to describe the Free Pepsi Dance. Suffice it to say, it comes from the soul . . . of hope fulfilled . . . of absolute victory and joy. If you have ever had your emotions explode in complete satisfaction and you danced, then you have done the Free Pepsi Dance.

A few minutes later, Jeff came on with the companion commercial, giving everyone instructions on how to get their free Pepsi Edge. We had to get online, go to a certain website, and we could print out the coupon. Never has an emotional state changed so rapidly. We went from "the thrill of victory" to the "agony of defeat" faster than anyone has ever experienced. WE DIDN'T HAVE INTERNET! NO coupon, NO free Pepsi. Every last bit of triumph was completely sucked out of the room. We were left with abject disappointment and disgust.

That night is one of my most cherished memories of time spent with my son. To this day, we laugh about what happened that evening, and any time there is great excitement, we break out in the Free Pepsi Dance. That said, there have been those times when I have had to discipline my kids, Kenneth in particular. He seemed to have gotten into more trouble than Emily as they were growing up. Regardless, the things that remain in my memory the most are the times of fun, the times of joy. Those moments of discipline, as real as they were, never really seem to hold my mind the way the times of joy do.

God is the same way. Does He discipline us? Of course He does: "For whom the Lord loves He reproves, even as a father corrects the son in whom he delights."[1] What I would like to point out is that as God disciplines, He also chooses to forgive and move forward in relationship. He doesn't get stuck on the judgment that He may have had to bring; instead, He is always looking for the joy that comes in redemption.

The book of Jeremiah contains a passage that has become one of my favorites and conveys this idea really well. Jeremiah was known as the weeping prophet because of the way he wept (go figure). His heart broke for the wickedness of the people of the kingdom of Judah and the judgment and captivity he knew that God would bring. He brought message after message, trying to bring the people to a place of repentance and to return to God, but they refused to listen.

When God calls Jeremiah to reach out to the southern kingdom of Judah, He starts off with what I find to be an encouraging word that underscores my point: "The word of the Lord came to me: 'Go and proclaim in the hearing of Jerusalem: "I remember the devotion of your youth, how as a bride you loved me and followed me through the desert, through a land not sown. Israel was holy to the Lord, the firstfruits of his harvest; all who devoured her were held guilty, and disaster overtook them," declares the Lord.'"[2]

This passage speaks of Israel's exodus and their time of wandering in the desert for forty years. I thought that was supposed to be a time of judgment... wasn't it? The reason wandered was because of their constant complaining and refusal to go into the Promised Land. They spurned God as incapable of being able to help them overcome the giants that lived in the land of Canaan. God was ready to destroy them all and start over with Moses; however, Moses' entreaty led the Lord to pardon the people and instead of destroying them, He had them wander for forty years until that generation died, and a new generation replaced the former one.[3]

Now in the passage above, God calls the desert wanderings a time of devotion on the people's part. He looks on it fondly and remembers the love they showed Him and the way they followed Him: "Israel was holy to the Lord." We tend to look on that time as a period of judgment. Yet when God tries to woo back the people of Jeremiah's day, He points out the great affection He shared with their forefathers in the desert experience.

Think about the implications from our perspective. If, indeed, the forty years were a time of God's anger, how would we feel? The Israelites lived out something that no other people in history has ever had, before or since—the direct, physical manifest presence of God leading and guiding them on a daily basis. From the time they crossed the Red Sea, the Lord led the people of Israel with a pillar of cloud by day and a pillar of fire by night. That pillar was a manifestation of the glory of God. When the Ark of the Covenant and tabernacle were completed, the cloud remained over the structure at the center of camp ALL the time, except for when Moses met with God at the special tent of meeting on the outskirts of the camp and when God was leading them to their next location.

The Hebrews could walk out of their tent at any time and see God's glory. Now I don't know about you, but if I knew that God was mad at me, I don't think I would be interested in seeing Him. I would probably try to avoid Him. How do you do that for *forty years*? I would never come out of my tent.

"Is He still out there?"

"Yup, still out there!"

"Well, I'm not going out there. He's ticked off." Instead of bringing the comfort of God's presence, the pillar would be a daily reminder of His displeasure and our impending doom. How unbearable!

Consider what things God did during this time for His people. At no time during their travels in the wilderness did the Lord cease to feed them. The manna God provided for them did not stop when He passed judgment on them for their forty-year sojourn. Through His loving kindness, He continued to feed His betrothed. Along with that, He performed the unique miracle of sustaining their sandals and clothes. They didn't wear out.[4] Does that sound like an angry God, or a God that loves, forgives, and moves forward?

Hopefully at this point in this book, you have learned that if you sin or mess up, the possibility exists that God *might* correct you. You have also learned that He *will* forgive you. What do I want you to see here? Even through the disappointment of failure and consequences, God still loves you. It is such a deep love that He chooses to forget the bad times and remember the good times He has shared with you. He desires to dance the Free Pepsi Dance with you. Will you dance with your Father?

## Think About It

- The Lord fed and clothed the Israelites in the desert. How has He demonstrated His love for you even when you thought He was angry at you?
- God wants to forgive you and move forward. What past failures are you holding onto that keep you from joining Him?

- What good times have you shared with your heavenly Father?

# CHAPTER SIX

# Stupid Faith

# or

# A Lesson from Economics

I know. I probably lost a lot of you with the word *Economics* in the title. Just stick with me for a little bit, and I will make it worth your while. After all, we are talking about finances. If it really is that difficult of a subject, feel free to send me as much of your money as you would like if it will help you through this chapter.

Money can be spent three ways. The first way is known as a First Party Payer. This involves spending your own money in order to get something you want or need. This is, by far, the most efficient way to spend money. Whenever a person buys something with their own money, they are usually—*usually*—very careful how they spend it. Because they know exactly what they want, they will take the time to get the best value for that item. If what they want is not available, often they will wait until it is or will purchase something else that's nearly identical to what they wanted, especially for a big-ticket item.

The last vehicle I bought was a mid-sized SUV. I knew I couldn't get a full-sized one because it would bust the budget, and I really didn't want to experience the joys of a repo. At the same time, a regular car just wouldn't meet the needs of my family. I went to various dealerships and made comparisons across makes and models in order to find something that was not only practical but something I truly wanted. Even after I had a vehicle picked out, I compared prices and options from one dealership to another to get an even better deal. I took the time to spend my own money the way I wanted. *I* got an SUV *I* liked with features *I* wanted that would suit *my* family for the price *I* wanted to pay. When it was all done, *I* was satisfied as a First Party Payer.

The second possibility is called a Second Party Payer (it's true). In this particular method, someone else will spend their money on your behalf or for your benefit. Now I know that sounds a bit confusing, so let me give you an example of how Second Party Payer works.

As I think back, I was four years old during the first Christmas that I can remember. When I close my eyes, I can see everything that took place just as if it were yesterday. I remember walking into my parents' bedroom along with my older brother and sister. It was time to wake the big people up and go open the presents. As the gifts were being passed out, my mom called me over. She handed me a small, nicely wrapped box and told me to go give it to my dad because this particular present was from me. I was so excited! I had something to give to my dad! I ran over and practically threw it at him as I gleefully shouted, "This is from me!" My dad made a big deal of the whole thing. He smiled, gave me a big hug, and thanked me for his present. At that moment, I believe I was more anxious to see what was in that box than my father was. That's because I had NO IDEA what I had given him.

Is Second Party Payer beginning to make sense? No four-year-old child has the wherewithal or the means to go to the store, pick out a gift, pay for it, wrap it, and see to it that Santa Claus makes sure it gets under the tree. My mother had been the one to take the time to pick out something my father would like, pay for it, and make sure it was ready for him on Christmas morning. She did all the work and spent the money, but it was for my benefit and on my behalf. The same kind of thing still happens today. Typically when a gift is needed for someone in my wife's family, she will do all the work making sure they get it, but will still sign my name to the card and package along with hers. I do the same thing when it comes to my family.

This model is not as efficient as the first. The person doing the shopping will certainly be careful with the way they spend their money; however, it may be that the payer spends less or maybe even more on the item than you might have. Along with that is the idea that what they pick out might not be what you would have chosen. If I remember correctly, "I" had given my dad some cologne that Christmas long ago. However, had I done the shopping, I am POSITIVE that my father would have much preferred a GI Joe than some dumb old bottle of smelly stuff.

Now we come to the last means, the Third Party Payer. This is, without a doubt, the worst way to spend money. It is rife with waste and in ongoing circumstances can lead to gross corruption. A Third Party Payer is when someone else spends your money on your behalf or for your benefit (supposedly).

It's lunchtime at work and I'm starving. I ask one of my co-workers, Gene, to go pick something up for me to eat and give him a $50 bill (OBVIOUSLY this is a fictitious illustration). My stomach screams at me and considering the amount of money I gave to Gene, I expect something substantial when he returns. My mind goes to Outback curbside pick-up: a nice steak with mashed potatoes, a salad, and maybe even one of their blooming onions.

However, when Gene returns, I am sorely disappointed. He went to a fast-food place and ordered items off the dollar menu for me. I have a small burger, a small fry, and a small drink. When I ask Gene for my change, he informs me that on the way back, he saw a homeless guy standing in the median with a sign, declaring his great need. Gene, being the good Christian brother that he is, wanted to help this man out, so he gave him my 47 dollars in change.

Sounds a bit over the top, doesn't it? Yet it is the kind of thing the governments around the world do every day. For the calendar year 2003, the US Federal government cannot account for $24.5 BILLION. How do you lose $24,500,000,000.00?[1] I'm sure you have heard of the earmark spending items that get stuffed into the various bills, such items like the $1.75 million given to both the University of Missouri and Purdue University in 2000 for animal waste research.

Then there was the $1.5 million for the refurbishment of the Vulcan Statue in Birmingham, Alabama in 2001, which was subsequently raised to an even $2 million in 2002. What—they didn't fix it right the first time?

In 2009, 1.9 million taxpayer dollars were spent for a water taxi service to Pleasure Beach, Connecticut, which has a population of 0![2] Legislators are happy to spend your money on their pet projects for your "benefit." Yet the only ones who ever seem to really get anything out of these schemes are the politicians themselves as they get reelected term after term, only to spend more money that doesn't belong to them. We might as well roll up our money and smoke it. No, wait, we dealt with that in chapter one.

Do you see the wretched model of Third Party Payer? Do you see how much abuse and corruption creeps in when the one doing the spending really has no vested interest in either the capital or the product? Next time you have the chance, do a search on your computer for government waste or earmarks. The number of sites and articles that comes up will blow your mind (although if you are the kind of person that is prone to anger, you may want to wait until after you have read through chapter ten, "Stupid Anger").

As bad as it is, Third Party Payer is the way that God works the most. On an almost daily basis, I hear people remark how they believe in God, but rarely have I heard them speak to the truth of how God believes in them. The ultimate example of this is the Great Commission: "Go therefore and make disciples of all the nations . . ."[3] and "Go into all the world and preach the gospel to all creation . . . "[4] Jesus was raised from the dead. That was the ultimate proof of His message of forgiveness and reconciliation with God. He fulfilled His purpose in redeeming mankind. What does He do? He ascends to heaven! If you want something done right, you are supposed to do it yourself. Not Jesus. Instead of staying on earth to be His own living proof, He leaves the job of spreading the good news of the gospel with His disciples and the church. He believes in us so much that He commits to *us* the fulfillment of His mission.

The parable of the talents gives us an even more personal image of God's faith in us.[5] Three servants are given varying amounts of money to hold onto while their lord goes on a journey. At the end of the parable, the lord comes back to find out just how the servants used the funds that had been left in their charge. In the same way, God has given all of us talents, skills, and abilities, and He has turned us loose on the world to see just how we will use them. Like in the parable, some people have more talents than others, but that is not the point. The point is that there is no such thing as someone having **no gifts**. Jesus will return someday. When He does, He will take the time to examine us to see how we have used the talents He gave us. God has faith in you. He believes in you. That is why He Third Party pays the gifts He has faithfully entrusted to you so that you can bless your community and the world.

## Think About It

- What gifts and talents has God given to you? (Determining what you like to do and are good at can help you figure this out.)
- How are you using your gifts to help with the Great Commission?
- How are you using your gifts to impact the people around you?
- How does knowing that God has faith in you inspire you?

# CHAPTER SEVEN

# Stupid Planning

# or

# That Don't Make No Sense

Life can't always be happy. It sure enough doesn't always make sense. As a minister, I can tell you that I have done more funerals than I can remember. Of the countless services I have officiated, participated in, or attended, I have only kept programs from four of them.

The first was for a little girl named Kellie Michelle Hix. I was a senior in high school when she lost her fight with cancer. She was only ten years old. Her sister, Kendra, was a junior, and I knew her fairly well.

We attended Camp Springs Christian School, a small school that ran from kindergarten through twelfth grade. Kellie was easy to pick out from the other kids, especially towards the end. Over time, she became more and more frail. I remember her having to use crutches to get around, and she wore a wig to cover the loss of her hair due to cancer treatments. She passed away on Thursday, March 6, 1986. Even though everyone who knew her understood the inevitability of her passing, it still came as a shock. The death of one so young is never the kind of thing you can really prepare for. Her funeral was held that Saturday. It was amazing how many from the school attended.

The fourth program was for Courtney Lynn Cody. Courtney's funeral was one of the last things I did at the end of my five-year tenure as the pastor in Spray, Oregon. It was an incredibly difficult and emotional funeral to do. She was only sixteen years old.

Courtney had been dealing with some rather serious pain issues; and early one morning, she had taken some medication to help alleviate her discomfort. Unfortunately, the medication made her vomit as she slept. She asphyxiated on it—never really having the chance to wake up and fight for her life. The Spray ambulance crew fought for her. I drove the ambulance. I will never forget those desperate moments in her bedroom as different members of the squad took turns doing CPR, trying to bring her back to life. Her father and mother, Rob and Nita, cried and begged for her to come back. Part of the tragedy was that her father had checked on her not even an hour prior to their frantic call to 911. How often do we miss the passing of an hour? Somewhere in that short sixty minutes, their baby girl lost her struggle for life, and their lives would never be the same.

The EMTs made the decision to call air life and have Courtney medevac'd to the hospital in Prineville. She would be under a doctor's care in mere minutes. Rob and Nita started the eighty-mile drive to the hospital, still clinging to the hope that their only daughter would pull through. *I* helped wheel her out of the house, and *I* helped put her in the ambulance while the EMTs continued their valiant efforts to save her. *I* drove her to the landing zone where the air life helicopter would come to pick her up. *I* helped put her on the chopper while the air life crew took over the fight for Courtney. As the *ambulance driver*, all of those things were my responsibility.

As I prepared to leave town and meet the Codys in Prineville, I received a call from the hospital, letting me know that Courtney hadn't survived. In order to beat her parents to the hospital, I drove at breakneck speed through the mountains. *I would be the one to tell them the horrible news.* I had to lean Rob against the walls to keep him from collapsing to the floor when I told him. As their *pastor*, that was my responsibility.

It should be noted that Spray is a town of 150 people in a county of only 2,000. Suffice it to say, it's the kind of place where everyone knows everyone. The two previous pastors who knew the Cody family came and assisted with the service. Courtney's funeral was huge. It was a time of unbearable heartbreak and anguish for the entire community.

The second program was from a funeral I didn't even attend. It was for a ten-year-old boy by the name of Brian Andrew Washington-Davis*. Although Brian and his family attended a different church, Brian would come to the children's group I was running on Wednesday nights at Ossining Gospel Assembly in Ossining, New York.

I drove the church van, and sometimes it took up to three trips to transport all the children to and from church for service. Brian was a boy like any other in the kid's program, and on any given night, you could count on one of the little rascals to become a bit rambunctious. I had to have some form of discipline in place, or I'd lose control. It was not unusual to have to give a few warnings to some of the kids each Wednesday, but if one of them was out of hand, I would suspend them for a week. They had to take a suspension form home, explaining why they had to stay out for a week. The child could not return unless the form had been signed by a parent. Whenever I gave one of these out, the kid would invariably cry and then yell, "I'm never coming back!" That never happened. Every time a child was suspended, they sat out a week, and when they were eligible to return, they would be standing on the sidewalk with a big smile on their face, waving their signed form in the air as I pulled up in the van.

You guessed it: Brian got suspended. Like all the others who had been suspended, he did his time and was back in church two weeks later. I didn't always do a salvation appeal, but the night Brian returned, I felt led by the Spirit to do one. When I presented the opportunity, Brian and one other girl raised their hands in response to the offer to ask Jesus into their lives. My wife took them into the next room to lead them in prayer while I closed that night's meeting.

It is always exciting when a person takes that step of faith to trust the Lord. This one was a bit unusual in that when my wife and I got home that night, she said she really grilled the two kids on just what they were doing. She wasn't sure why she had done that since it wasn't her normal practice. She took *extra* time to make sure they understood Jesus' death and resurrection and the forgiveness He offers by simply asking for it. They were clear on what they were doing when they asked Jesus into their lives.

Two weeks later, Brian was dead. It was Sunday morning, June 26, 1994, and we were kicking off a week long tent-style revival and children's outreach. As I left my office and made my way to the tent we had set up on the church grounds, one of the little girls came running up to me shouting, "Did you hear about Brian? He drowned in the river yesterday!" I thought she was joking, but it was validated by the dozen or so other kids who had come with her. One of them showed me a clipping from the morning paper. Brian and a few friends had gone down to the river to swim, and while swimming underwater, his foot became lodged under some stones. He never resurfaced. The featured photo showed a boat and some divers trying to recover his body. Another little boy was sitting on the bank with a blanket wrapped around his shoulders. I recognized him as another of the children that attended our youth group. I was heartbroken. I was useless for the entire morning's service.

When Monday morning came, I focused on pulling myself together, throwing myself into the preparations for the children's outreach that night. I also kept trying to make contact with Brian's family and pastor. That's when I got the phone call from my mother. My older brother, Alan, was missing. He was a pilot flying for Missionary Aviation Fellowship in Venezuela, and his plane had gone down in the jungle. That was all we knew.

I had to work. I couldn't think about any of this...it was all just too much. There were things that I needed to do for that night's service, and I focused the whole of my mind on them. About an hour later, my wife came and told me my mother had called. Alan hadn't made it.

The rest of the day passed in a blur. Venezuelan law required that the body be buried as soon as possible. If I was going down there, I had to leave immediately. By mid-afternoon, I was on a plane to Miami. The next morning, I picked up an emergency expedited passport from the state department, and that afternoon I boarded a plane bound for Caracas, Venezuela. Genevieve, my wife, took my place at Brian's funeral service. When I returned, she had a program for me.

When I finally got to Venezuela, I heard the full story about my brother. Alan had been transporting a local pastor with several jerry cans of gasoline and some large tanks of propane in the belly pod and cabin. The village airstrip ended on a river that meandered through the jungle. Witnesses said the plane sounded odd as it tried to take off and used 90% of the runway. It shouldn't have even needed 50%. The plane leapt into the sky, barely clearing the trees on the other side of the river. Then, just as rapidly as it had taken off, it fell out of the sky.

As it came down, a tree tore the left wing open, spilling fuel everywhere. The aircraft spun 180 degrees and hit the ground flat. The ensuing fireball could be seen back in the village one hundred feet up in the air over the tops of the trees. There was so much fuel that even after the other MAF pilots flew out to the village, got in a canoe, and traveled several bends in the river to the crash site, it was still on fire.

After the funeral, my father and I went out to the site. The conflagration had consumed nearly the entire plane. All that remained were portions of the wings, the tail with about three feet worth of the fuselage, and, ironically enough, the engine. The plane hit so hard that the engine was buried in the earth with the top of it below ground level. I sifted through the dirt where Alan would have been seated and found his four-point seatbelt still clasped but now also fused by the heat of the fire. I still have it today.

There was nothing left of my brother but bones. We laid him to rest in the land where he gave his life for the Lord's calling. He was buried in a flimsy metal coffin. I was one of six pall bearers but, truth be told, the other five weren't needed. So little remained of Alan and so light was his coffin that I could have carried it myself.

My father and I flew back to the U.S. together while my mom stayed behind and helped my brother's wife, Therese. Alan was only thirty years old. He left behind a wife and three kids, ages two, five, and nine. Considering a two-year mission's degree, flight and mechanical training, language school, and itinerating to raise support, it had taken ten years to get to the mission field. He was there for one year. Pops, my Dad, is a good man, not given to swaying emotions. Sitting next to him in that plane while he wept was more than I could bear. We held a memorial service for Alan when everyone was back in the country—hence, the third of my four programs.

The loss that death brings is painful, but these deaths all seemed like such a waste. How could any of this be God's plan? THAT DON'T MAKE NO SENSE! I wouldn't have allowed these things to happen. Three were just kids and the fourth, Alan, served the Lord. After a thorough investigation, they could find no cause for the crash. How could any of this show God's glory? How could any of this possibly be attributed to a God that claims to be good? The heart of these questions and the problems they pose are ultimately summed up in the question, "WHY?"

That is the most vexing question any of us can ask and, in my experience, it is often the question God

leaves unanswered. Trying to find purpose in the
darkest of tragedies is what I have found to be the
greatest cause of loss of faith in the Lord. We all want to
know the purpose behind loss. We search for an
explanation. When we don't get one, we speculate and
try to affix some rationale of our own that will assuage
our hurt and give us reasons to keep moving forward.

Such an instance exists in the gospel of John. On
the night of Jesus' betrayal, one of His closest disciples,
Peter, denies Jesus three times. The Bible tells us that
Peter wept bitterly over his denial. After His
resurrection, Jesus restored and forgave Peter by asking
him three times, "Do you love me?" After Peter affirms
his love for Jesus a third time, Jesus moves the
conversation to a difficult place:

> 'Truly, truly, I say to you, when you were
> younger, you used to gird yourself and walk
> wherever you wished; but when you grow old,
> you will stretch out your hands and someone
> else will gird you, and bring you where you do
> not wish to go.' Now this He said, signifying by
> what kind of death he would glorify God. And
> when He had spoken this, He said to him, 'Follow
> Me!' Peter, turning around, saw the disciple

whom Jesus loved following them; the one who also had leaned back on His bosom at the supper and said, 'Lord, who is the one who betrays You?' So Peter seeing him said to Jesus, 'Lord, and what about this man?' Jesus said to him, 'If I want him to remain until I come, what is that to you? You follow Me!' Therefore this saying went out among the brethren that that disciple would not die; yet Jesus did not say that he would not die, but only, 'If I want him to remain until I come, what is that to you?'[1]

In this passage, Jesus not only restores Peter but lets him know that Peter will remain faithful to the end of his life—a martyr's end at that. When Jesus tells Peter to follow him, Peter notices John, another disciple, following along as well. So Peter asks Jesus, "What about him?" Isn't that like all of us? It's not enough to hear from the Lord for our own lives. We have to know what God plans on doing with others.

Jesus' answer still did not do enough to abate the curiosity of those that remained after His ascension: "If I want him to remain until I come, what is that to you? You follow Me!" The passage tells us that some in the church believed that John would not die before Jesus returned. Can you imagine the panic and confusion that erupted when John did die, and Jesus had apparently not returned? Or perhaps Jesus did return and they missed it! All of this was based on speculation that sprung from a misinterpretation of what Jesus said, along with their plain "nosiness."

If I may, allow me to translate Jesus' words to Peter in a modern vernacular: "Peter, I know you love John, but I don't want you to worry about him. Let me take care of him. You don't need to involve yourself in the deeper details of his life because there will be plenty of things in your own life to keep you busy. Just follow me and rest assured that I will take care of you, too." How hard that is for us to swallow. We are a bunch of nosy busybodies that like to be in the thick of the Lord's business as he works in the lives of others. If the person in question happens to be family, well that means we should have been included in the conversation and planning. Right? Wrong! Let's be honest about something: we have a difficult enough time hearing from God for ourselves. So why should we expect to be God's counselor when it comes to others?

The people in your life are going to die, and one day, you will too. If you haven't lost someone close to you yet, rest assured, someday you will. Death comes to us all, and you will want answers. I wanted to know the answers for Kellie, Courtney, Brian, and Alan. I loved those people. They were dear to me. But are they not dear to the Lord as well? He loves them with a love that I can never hope to match. Not only that, but God is eternal. He sees and understands things on an infinite level. My existence in this world is temporal  I can hardly see past today. I trust God, and I have also come to the place where I realize that I am probably not going to get a full understanding of the questions I have concerning those four (among others) until I also take that leap to the other side. If I turn to speculation—or worse, to bitterness—it will only hamper my ability to follow the Lord.

## Think About It

- Have you experienced the loss of a loved one?
- How are you dealing with (or how did you deal with) the feelings of loss?
- Can you, or have you, let them go, and are you trusting God for the answers "someday"?
- Do you think the loss and the need for answers are getting in your way of following Jesus?

# CHAPTER EIGHT

# Stupid Predicaments
# or
# Life Out of Control

Some things in life are just way beyond our control. It seems that no matter what we do to prevent them, circumstances we can't do anything about arise. I had just such an occasion when I worked at the Clerk of the Court's office—yes, the same office mentioned in a previous chapter.

Our main court building was not big enough to handle all of the cases and hearings that came in, so for that reason, we sometimes went down the street to the District Court to use its courtroom. Unfortunately, this courtroom was rife with mold. This wasn't just any garden variety mold either . . . try neurotoxic. Although we didn't know it at the time, we later discovered that exposure to this mold caused memory, vision, thinking, and motor skill problems. These symptoms were cropping up in everyone who spent any extended time in that building, but it took a long time before anyone figured out the missing link.

We eventually began to question whether or not the building could be the root issue, so the clerk found a doctor to examine us. Unfortunately, since I spent more time in that building than anyone else in our office, my symptoms were more severe.

Because of the symptoms I exhibited, the doctor slated me for a battery of tests, including a CT scan. I'd always been in good health, so I had no idea what to expect from this. He scheduled the appointment with a local hospital, and off I went.

To prepare for the test, I could not eat or drink anything after midnight the night before. I have a high-speed metabolism, so by the time I arrived for my 9 AM appointment, I was pretty hungry. While I filled out the necessary paperwork, one of the nurses disappeared into the back. When she returned, she was holding phase one of my CT scan—an empty cup and a container with nearly two quarts of a milky-looking liquid, but it sure enough wasn't milk. She poured some of the container's contents into the cup, and as she handed it to me, she said it had a nice vanilla taste. She then told me I had to drink *all* of the container's contents. After the first cup, that "nice vanilla taste" was long gone. Not only that, but the consistency went down like liquid chalk. This stuff coats a person's insides so the CT scan can detect any problems with the digestive tract.

After the second cup, I knew it was not going to be fun, so I tried to down the goop as fast as I could—until I burped, that is. I nearly threw up. It tasted twice as bad coming back up, and the stickiness of the drink rose to a whole new level. Only halfway through the container, I knew I had to change my approach. No way would I start this process over, so what went down had to stay down! I slowed down my gulping pace, and although the last couple of cups were absolutely grueling, I managed to hold it in.

I was hoping for a moment's respite, but as soon as I finished choking down the last disgusting cup, the nurse came back and asked me to follow her. She led me towards the back of the hospital for phase two. This time, she was carrying one of those little hospital gowns. We stopped in front of a small room, and as she handed it to me, she said, "Take everything off and put this on. The CT Tech will be with you in just a few moments."

Hmmmm. I stepped into the room and closed the door. I thought, "Does she mean *everything* everything, or everything-but-my-underwear everything?" The garment would tell me. If it tied on the side, then I knew I could keep my underwear. If it tied in the back . . . it *did* tie in the back. I took off *everything* everything, put on the garment, took a seat, and tried to keep my "breakfast" down.

After a while, the tech showed up and directed me to my ultimate destination. The tech told me to take a seat on the machine's bench and then began to explain the variety of things that would be done to me. First, I was given an explanation of the machine itself: after lying down on a small bed, I would be moved in and out of this incredibly narrow tube as it whirred and banged and made all kinds of noise. Along with that, I had to lie perfectly still and hold my breath as instructed.

Next, I would be hooked up to an IV full of some kind of dye. Yay, I got to be poked. I don't particularly mind needles, but after what I had been through so far, I was not quite in the mood. This dye would reveal my entire circulatory system and show if there was anything wrong with my blood flow. It had some interesting side effects. As the dye coursed through my veins, it would "heat me up" (and believe me, it did. At its peak, I felt as though I was going to spontaneously combust). Not only that, but sometimes people have extreme allergic reactions to the dye; however, I was told, "Don't worry—I'll be standing by. If you begin to have a reaction, I will shoot an antihistamine into your IV." Wow, it just keeps getting better and better.

What came next, however, was the cake topper, the piece de resistance, the coup de grace. The liquid I drank earlier was for an Upper GI, something to see the top end of my digestive system. What was also needed was a Lower GI, something to see the "back end" of my digestive system. The tech informed me that an IV bag full of liquid, presumably the same kind of stuff I drank only minus the flavoring, would also have to be administered, and that *she* would give it to me via an enema, and that I would have to hold it until the test was done. Yeah, that's right, the tech was a SHE! The only thing going right for me was that I had guessed right about the garment and "everything."

How did it come to this? I was just doing my job. It was just mold, for crying out loud. This had spun way out of control, yet nothing else could be done about it. There was no point in whining if I wanted to find out what was making me sick. Well, BRING IT ON!

We may be living *our* lives, but sometimes things beyond our control and our understanding broadside us. King David experienced just such a set of circumstances. How he handled his predicament is an excellent lesson for all of us.

It all started with King Saul's obsession to kill him. Even though David had proven himself to be completely loyal to the king, Saul's jealousy drove him to hunt David like an animal. David was his son-in-law, yet Saul forced him and all his men to live in the wild, continuously running for their lives. Eventually, David, his followers, and their families all took refuge with the Philistines, the sworn enemies of the Israelites.[1] Remember the story of David and Goliath? Yeah, Goliath was a Philistine.

David spent several years with the Philistines, and he lived under the supervision of a particular lord named Achish who had generously given David and his people the city of Ziklag to inhabit. Eventually, though, another conflict arose between Israel and the Philistines. King Saul marched out with his armies for a showdown with the Philistine kings. David marched out in league with King Achish and his Philistine warriors to fight against King Saul. When the other Philistine lords and kings arrived at the rally point, they very wisely instructed Achish to send David and his men home. They weren't about to give David a chance to possibly get into Saul's good graces by turning on them.[2] What a soap opera. David just can't seem to catch a break. And it's just about to get worse.

After a three-day journey back to their hometown, Ziklag, David and his men arrived to a scene of horror and destruction. The Amalekites had raided the city and literally carried off everyone and everything. Anything not nailed down was taken, and what they could not carry, they burned. The city had been reduced to rubble: "When David and his men came to the city, behold, it was burned with fire, and their wives and their sons and their daughters had been taken captive. Then David and the people who were with him lifted their voices and wept until there was no strength in them to weep."[3] Talk about despair. As if it couldn't get any worse, it did. David's men ended up blaming him for the catastrophe, and they started talking about stoning him.

David, however, did not allow these circumstances to dictate his attitudes or actions. He didn't sit around or give up. He certainly didn't let those he was surrounded by intimidate him; instead, "David strengthened himself in the Lord his God."[4] He reached down into his soul and hit the reset button for his faith in God. Then, David called for the priest Abiathar in order to inquire of the Lord.

God instructed David to pursue the Amalekites. This was no small feat. It took several days just to catch up with them. The journey was so arduous that 200 of his 600 men fell behind due to exhaustion. Upon finding the Amalekite army, David's small band immediately engaged them in battle. The fight raged from the evening of one day to the evening of the next—a full 24 hours. A mere 400 of the Amalekites escaped, and that's only because they mounted their camels and lit out. When all was said and done, not only did David's men capture the spoils of the Amalekites' other raids, but everyone and everything that had been taken from Ziklag was recovered, from the youngest child to the smallest lamb. Nothing was missing.[5]

You can be assured that life will take some twists and turns, and you will never see them coming until it's too late. Just because circumstances get beyond your control, it doesn't mean you have to be out of control during times of crisis and challenge. David strengthened himself in the Lord. We have to learn how to do the same thing. You will be amazed at the courage you will find when you dig deep inside and find the faith you need to overcome the challenges that stare you in the face. Search the Scriptures and spend time in prayer. Seeking God is the key. He can bring control not only to you but to the predicaments that overwhelm you.

## Think About It

- What is the most unpredictable thing you have ever faced?
- What was your reaction to the circumstances?
- How did the situation turn out?
- Did you ask God for help?
    - If you did, how did He help you?
    - If you didn't, how do you think things might have gone differently if you had?

# CHAPTER NINE

## Stupid Pride

## or

## Volleyball is a Cruel, Cruel Game

Some people just seem to have it all going for them: good looks, athletic ability, intelligence, money, popularity . . . the list goes on. Unfortunately, when I was growing up, I was not one of those people. In fact, I really didn't have strength in any of these areas. If you saw me, nothing about my appearance would lead you to believe that I might be the next big movie or TV star. I played soccer in junior high and high school . . . well, I warmed the bench. In fact, in tenth grade, I didn't even make the team. At the same time, I was the only kid in my family to ever bring home a failing grade on a report card. Ninth grade was an absolute horror show—I nearly failed. Thank God for choir—my only A! I was kind of nerdy without the benefit of having the brains to go with the moniker. I have never had a lot of money, and no one was beating a path to my door to spend any time with me or seek my advice. I was abundantly average as a teenager (and sometimes below average).

In twelfth grade, an opportunity to finally gain some recognition presented itself, and I jumped all over it. It was homecoming, and the school was having a school-wide pep rally. The seniors on the girls' varsity volleyball team challenged the seniors on the boys' varsity soccer team to a match. Even though I wasn't a starter, they invited me to play, and I was more than eager.

The pep rally and game were going to be held on Friday, so we had all week to talk smack, and I did more than my fair share. I went to a small Christian school: my graduating class had 41 students. The entire student body would be in the gym to witness the beating the boys were going to give to the girls. I made sure that everybody knew I was going to be a part of the show. There was no humility in the pre-game bravado and certainly no sense that this was all "just for fun."

It has been said that revenge is a dish best served cold. I would also contend that humble pie is a dish best served in front of a lot of people. Now, it's not what you think. The boys won the game as we said we would. The pie was not for us as a group. It was going to be a single slice, with my name written on it in whipped cream capital letters.

When the game began, I started in the server's position. I had a decent serve and scored several points for our team. Serving and taking my turn on the back line was not the issue. My moment of truth came as we went through the rotation, and I found myself in center position on the front line.

I can see it all clearly as if it were yesterday. My classmate, Sean Cranford, stood on my right. (That is how indelibly seared into my mind this whole event is.) The girls had the service. The server aimed for the back row. The player bumped the ball to Sean. As it arced its way to Sean, he looked at me, called my name, and delivered a perfect set. It was absolutely beautiful. It was a moment made for great glory.

# Stupid Pride or Volleyball is a Cruel, Cruel Game

My time had come. One of the girls would be going home with AMF Voit imprinted on her forehead. I was about to lay down the queen mother of all spikes. Over that week, I had declared the impending doom that would be realized on the volleyball court, and now was the time to make good on my boast.

Sean's pass hung gracefully in the air. Because he stood to my right, I was already in the perfect position since I'm right handed. The set was played so well, I didn't even have to move. All I had to do was leap up, and lay it down. Time slowed as I jumped with every bit of strength I could muster. "Air" Jordan would have been impressed with my height and hang time. I swung my arm with extreme prejudice and malice aforethought, and missed. Not the kind of miss where you graze the ball and it goes out of bounds. The kind of miss where all you get is a handful of nothing. In slow motion, I watched my hand go by the ball into the emptiness that became my disgrace.

I was stunned. *I missed?! HOW COULD I MISS?! EVERYTHING WAS PERFECT!* That's when gravity took over and pulled me back to earth, down to my new reality. If only that were the end, but my piece of humble pie was about to get a little bigger. You see, I wasn't the only thing gravity was working on; it was also having an effect on the ball. Just when I thought things could get no worse, the volleyball, the implement of my pride, came down and bounced squarely on top of my head. The look on Sean's face betrayed a mix of shock, disbelief, and a smile. His expression said, "I can't believe what I just saw. Better you than me!" All the guys on the team mobbed me and not in celebration. The gym echoed with laughter.

What do you do after something like that? There's no point in getting mad, and you really better not cry. I raised my fists in mocking triumph and laughed along. There is a big difference between the helpless embarrassment of the previous chapter's CT scan, and the humiliation I was enjoying at this point. Really, I had asked for it with my braggadocios manner that week. Pride had run its full course, and now, I got to relish in its reward. Even though they may not know where it comes from, most people have heard the biblical proverb, "Pride goes before destruction, a haughty spirit before a fall."[1]

God really doesn't like pride. I mean *really* doesn't like it. In three separate places, the Bible says that He mocks and opposes the proud but gives favor and grace to the humble.[2] The Lord deliberately makes things difficult for the proud. I don't know about you, but the prospect of having God set against me isn't all that appealing. Why does He do that? Because proud people have a way of robbing everyone of their dignity and humanity. Have you ever known a nice, considerate, polite, and thoughtful person who was also proud? Of course not—that's a contradiction. You can't be interested in the welfare and well-being of others when you are consumed with getting your own way.

Jesus told his disciples several times that if they wanted to lead, then they had to serve. The gospel of Luke tells of one of those occurrences: "And there arose also a dispute among them as to which one of them was regarded to be the greatest. And He said to them, 'The kings of the Gentiles lord it over them; and those who have authority over them are called "Benefactors." But it is not this way with you, but the one who is the greatest among you must become like the youngest, and the leader like the servant. For who is the greater, the one who reclines at the table or the one who serves? Is it not the one who reclines at the table? But I am among you as the one who serves.'"[3]

Jesus leaves no room for self-promotion or aggrandizement. Pride does not allow you to serve, and Jesus is all about serving others. Instead of looking to put on a fun show for the school with my classmates, I walked into that gym with the goal of dishing out humiliation to make myself look good. I walked out of that gym humbled and wiser.

## Think About It

- When and how have you let your pride get the best of you?
- How did the Lord "help" you with your pride?
- In what areas of your life is it difficult to keep your pride in check?
- What are you doing to stay humble and esteem others?

# CHAPTER TEN

# Stupid Anger
# or
# Mess with the Bull, and
# You'll Get the Horns

Now I don't know about you, but I've found that
when I lose my temper, the results are disastrous. Let's
be clear. There is a difference between an anger that is
justifiable and when someone totally flips out—
between standing for what is right so that God is
revealed as good as opposed to defending our own
honor, position, or agenda. There's nothing like seeing
someone lose their cool. Raw anger has a way of
demeaning anyone and everyone that might be on the
receiving end. It has a way of making a mess of every-

thing. Think of it like emotional vomit. Usually when this happens, we don't get to see the end result for the person who vented their wrath, only those who were left to clean up the aftermath. Let me tell you, there are *always* repercussions for the person who loses his or her temper—it just isn't always evident to us. I once witnessed the boomerang come back and hit the one that threw it.

This event took place during the time I was pastoring in Oregon, and it happened at a branding (I'll tell you more about brandings in chapter twelve). We had managed to sort all of the calves from their mothers and had them all in one pen. Throughout the morning, we would take a few out of the pen and send them through the chute to be "worked." There were several dozen, so as we worked them, the smaller ones born later in the year were taken first. These calves can often be moved with a simple shout and wave of your hands. When that doesn't work, you can literally push them around and make them go where you want. If all else fails, you can wrestle them down, pick them up, and carry them to the chute.

It was now down to the last stubborn few, and these were nearly yearlings. A calf can put on a lot of weight in a year's time, so the last of the bunch were nothing to mess with. They are often fairly stubborn, so the shout doesn't work that well—they're wise to that trick. Because of their size, they also don't push too well either. Great care has to be taken around a larger calf because they have learned how to kick. That may not sound like much, but those of you who have taken a back hoof to the shin or the inside of the knee know the respect you had better show these animals. The rest of you who haven't . . . well, imagine letting a third grader pop you in the leg with a baseball bat. It's no laughing matter—unless, of course, it's happening to someone else.

It came to the point where we had sorted all but one. When I say we, I mean that there were six of us in the pen doing the sorting. One of "us" was a bona fide cowboy who I will call Fred. Fred had the build of a professional jockey—he was a tiny man but no one to be trifled with. He knew how to cowboy, and I respected him for that. There were years of knowledge, experience, and understanding when it came to animals in that man's mind. He may have been small, but he could handle the largest of horses with ease and knew his business when it came to cattle. However, this one calf was giving all of us an absolute fit. This was Satan's calf.

The farthest corner of the pen was where the barn and one of the fence lines came together. In this corner, there was a small pile of hay, and this calf had made that hay its place of safety. Whenever one of us would approach "el Diablo," he would stand up and run around the pen in seemingly random directions towards various people. The one place he wouldn't run was where he was supposed to—down the chute. No matter how many of us chased him and attempted to intimidate him into going into the chute, he would not go. Then he would return to the hay pile and lie down again, mocking us. Frustration was building. He was the LAST one. We started getting desperate. When he ran again, we tried tackling him. One of us would try to grab him while a few others would pile on.

Did I mention this was Satan's calf? No matter how many of us tried to bring this animal down, we couldn't do it. When we'd wrap our arms around him, he would deliberately run into a fence post or the barn, crushing our arms between his girth and the unforgiving wood. He would go into these wild spins with hooves flailing or kick up his hind legs at us.

Sometimes, he would simply drag us around until we had been stomped and were forced to let go. Nearly everybody had been kicked.

Then, Fred's son got whacked. El Diablo delivered one particularly vicious kick to his knee and then returned to his safety zone. Fred had had enough. Fred got angry. Fred began to yell ... *at us!* He bellowed, "STOP CHASING IT!"

I thought, *What are you yelling at us for? We're the ones getting tromped.*

I didn't dare say it out loud. You know how it goes. Challenge a person who is in the middle of a meltdown, and you're asking for it. Believe me—Fred was in the middle of a **nuclear** meltdown.

He continued, "IF YOU WOULD LEAVE IT ALONE, IT WOULD GO WHERE IT IS SUPPOSED TO! ALL YOU ARE DOING IS MAKING THINGS WORSE! STOP YELLING! STOP CHASING IT! JUST STAND STILL!"

Respect the man of knowledge and experience. We all stood stock still where we were, and no one so much as uttered a peep. We all had the plain sense to keep our mouths shut. Coincidentally, we'd formed a semi-circle a good twenty yards away from the calf. Fred was at the very center of our line.

Then it happened. One of the most God-ordained things I have ever seen in my life took place. As we stood facing the calf, he slowly rose to his feet. El Diablo took a couple of steps forward, and then stopped as if he were examining us. It seemed like Fred was right. The calf may have had enough as well. All of a sudden, Satan's calf dropped his head into a charge position and broke into a full sprint, straight for Fred. Without slowing one bit, he ran headlong into Fred's stomach. Fred's hat went flying off as he was picked up off his feet, arms flailing. El Diablo flicked his neck, tossing Fred further in the air, and then slowed down just enough to allow gravity to do its work. Fred fell flat on his back with a thud. But it wasn't over. The calf then started running again and gave Fred a sound trampling for good measure. As soon as it was done, the calf turned around, went back to his corner, and lay down again. I wouldn't have believed it if I hadn't seen it with my own eyes.

Fred gingerly got up, muttering something under his breath no one could hear, while he dusted himself off and retrieved his hat. No one else moved or made a sound, and we certainly didn't laugh (although I will admit I *really* wanted to). Of the six people in the pen, el

Diablo put the physical beat down on the **one** that had put the anger-fueled verbal beat down on the rest of us. Perhaps el Diablo wasn't so evil after all. Now he was more like God's agent for inspiring and developing self-control, and I was beginning to like him.

Certain people in the Bible also had issues with anger. One of them, Moses, is one of the most revered of Bible characters. No one in history experienced a walk with the Lord the way Moses did. The Lord himself said of his special relationship with Moses, "Hear now my words: If there is a prophet among you, I, the Lord, shall make Myself known to him in a vision. I shall speak with him in a dream. Not so, with My servant Moses, He is faithful in all My household; With him I speak mouth to mouth, even openly, and not in dark sayings, and he beholds the form of the Lord. Why then were you not afraid to speak against My servant, against Moses?"[1] The passage later tells us, "Thus the Lord used to speak to Moses face to face, just as a man speaks to his friend."[2] WOW! How do you like that? Moses truly had something unique going on with the Lord.

Even though Moses was great and so was his walk with God, it doesn't mean that he did not have his flaws or struggles. In the early years of his life, we can

see the first flashes of his anger when he lived in Egypt.[3]
Moses was a Hebrew raised in Pharaoh's house, the king
of Egypt. One day, Moses sees an Egyptian taskmaster
beating a Hebrew slave. The Bible tells us, "So he
looked this way and that, and when he saw there was no
one around, he struck down the Egyptian and hid him in
the sand."[4] It was deliberate murder. Seeing his fellow
Hebrews suffer made him mad enough to kill. It would
also be his inability to control that burst of rage that
would keep Moses out of the Promised Land.

The Lord performed an interesting miracle for
the Israelites when they ran out of water in the desert.
Of course, it all started with some complaining on the
part of the masses because they did not have anything
to drink. God instructed Moses to get the staff that had
been used to perform the miracles during their
deliverance from Egypt. He told Moses and the elders to
go out in plain sight of all the Israelites and approach a
certain rock on Mt. Horeb. Once they did so, God told
Moses to strike the rock with his staff, and when he did,
water came rushing out. Through Moses, the Lord
brought clean, drinkable water out of a boulder for the
entire nation of Israel.[5]

Although God provided this water for the Israelites, He punished them for complaining and refusing to enter the Promised Land by having them wander the desert for forty years (they had complained about other things as well—this is merely one example). This entire generation died within those forty years because they were not allowed to enter the Promised Land—only their descendants could.

Well, forty years later, the new generation repeated the same sin of their forefathers: they complained rather vehemently about the lack of water—namely, God's lack of provision.[6] Moses and Aaron inquired of the Lord as to what they should do. Again, the Lord told Moses to grab his staff and go out to the rock. This time, however, He told Moses to speak to the rock instead of strike it. In frustration and anger, Moses said to the people, "Listen now, you rebels; shall we bring forth water for you out of this rock?"[7] Can you feel Moses' anger? He then struck the rock, not once but twice. Water burst forth on the second blow. Moses' rage got the best of him. He railed against the people and beat the rock instead of simply speaking to it.

The Lord had some bad news for Moses and Aaron: "Because you have not believed Me, to treat Me as holy in the sight of the sons of Israel, therefore you shall not bring this assembly into the land which I have given them."[8] Hmmmm. Which commandment did he break? I don't remember "Thou shalt not hit rocks with sticks" anywhere in the Bible. Yet, that is just what kept Moses and Aaron out of the Promised Land. The Lord clearly told Moses to speak to the rock, which was intended to meet the needs of the people. But what did Moses do? He *hit* the rock (twice) and *then* chastised the Israelites. The Lord was trying to show His grace to a new generation; instead, His provision and holiness were distorted through the filter of Moses' anger.

When Moses gave the final instructions to the people before he died, he was still angry about the whole affair. When they were on the verge of crossing over to the Promised Land, he told the Israelites that he'd asked the Lord to change His mind and allow him into the Promised Land.[9] Moses said, "But the Lord was angry with me on your account, and would not listen to me; and the Lord said to me, 'Enough! Speak to Me no more of this matter.'"[10] Wait. Did Moses just say, "The Lord was angry with me on *your* account"?! Sounds to me like the age-old excuse, "Look what you made me do!" Moses was barred from the Promised Land for something that *he* had done, not something the people had done. His anger still smoldered, and he placed blame on others instead of facing the truth: his uncontrolled rage had gotten the best of him. The price for his outburst was steep, indeed. It usually is.

Human anger will never bring about the will of God. The book of James says it this way: "But everyone must be quick to hear, slow to speak and slow to anger; for the anger of man does not achieve the righteousness of God."[11] Such anger is antithetical to God's purpose of displaying how good He is. In such cases, God has no choice but to correct the error. Believe me, if He will keep Moses out of the Promised Land for hitting a rock with a stick, He will have something to say to us when we lose our cool as well. Mess with the bull, and you **will** get the horns!!!

## Think About It

- When have you experienced the unbridled anger of another?
- How did that make you feel?

- When have you lost your temper with another?
- Put yourself in their shoes; how do you think they felt?
- What were the repercussions for you? For them?
- Have you tried to make amends for your outburst(s)?
- Knowing your triggers can help with anger. What are the things that set you off?

# CHAPTER ELEVEN

## Stupid People

## or

## There Are Some Real

## Weirdoes Out There

I love to watch people. I could spend hours at the mall sitting on a bench and just looking at the parade of humanity in all of its diversity as it walks by. Having spent sixteen years pastoring, I can tell you that there are all kinds of people in this world. Weirdness knows no bounds.

For example, in a group of friends I know, every last one of them has some kind of quirk. They are the most eclectic group I have ever known, and it amazes me that this dysfunctional bunch found each other and created their own community.

One of them is ADHHHHHHHD. This guy is beyond wired. It's like he lives entirely on a diet of sugar and caffeine. He has the shortest attention span, exacerbated by the constant need to move—and when I say move, I mean MOVE. There is never a moment's respite; instead, he literally bounces around from one activity to the next. You can always tell when he's been around because he leaves behind the devastation of a tornado in his wake.

This, of course, causes a lot of problems for the second member of this "family." With major OCD and anger issues, he needs everything to be in its place all the time. When the first guy is around, it's an obvious catastrophe. Not only that, but everything has to be done a certain way. If the rules and protocol aren't followed, he absolutely blows a gasket.

Then there's the depressed one. No matter what's going on, this guy remains unhappy. They could be enjoying a picnic in a field of butterflies under a rainbow, and he would find something wrong. It's as if he's made it his business to spread doom and gloom to the rest of the gang.

The constant haranguing of all that's wrong with the world doesn't help the one who lives in constant fear. The littlest one in this crew remains in such a state of terror that he shakes almost all of the time and speaks with a very pronounced stutter. Every little sound sets this guy off. Trees shaking in the wind send him running, let alone a thunderstorm. If things get too tense, he becomes nearly useless.

No group is complete without some kind of genius. The only problem with the brains of this outfit is that he's a total recluse. It's never difficult to find him because he rarely leaves his house. If a problem is too much for the gang, they go see this guy, and he almost always has the answer.

The only female of the collection is a single mom. You never ever hear a word about the dad. He literally doesn't exist. It's almost as if there is no father for her only child, a boy. Even with the dad not being around, you don't see the mom much either. Her son, who's significantly younger than all of the others, is often allowed to run free with this motley crew. What good mother would allow her kid to be influenced by such a hopeless lot? This little guy soaks up everything he sees, so it can only be expected that he's going to "learn" a lot from his time with his friends.

Now we come to the ring leaders. One has major addiction issues. All he ever thinks about involves getting his next fix. You have to give him credit, though, because he comes up with the most outrageous schemes to feed his habit. The only problem is that it often involves the others in his gang. Most everything he does is in pursuit of the object of his addiction.

The other ring leader lives in a fantasy world. His poor soul must be tormented, having to choose the reality afforded by his mind over the reality afforded by life itself. Rarely do you ever see him making a foray into the realm of the normal. He spends countless hours in the woods, talking to imaginary people. The name of this place is the Hundred Acre Woods.

Yes, you guessed it. This outcast group of the weird and strange is none other than Christopher Robin and the cast of A.A. Milne's *Winnie the Pooh*. I'm sure you can now figure out what each character's "problem" is, but here's the answer key just in case: Tigger is the ADHHHHHHD individual that can't sit still for a single minute. Rabbit is the obsessive/compulsive one that would give Adrian Monk a run for his money. Eeyore, of course, cannot lift himself out of his depressive funk to save his life. Poor little Piglet is so wrapped up in fear, he often times can't figure out what to do with himself. Owl is the brainiac recluse that can't bring himself to leave his home. Kanga is the single mom of Roo, her unsupervised wild child. Pooh is the poor slob whose addiction to honey has caused more problems than it has ever solved. And the hopeless child who is so desperate for friends that he has to make them up from among his stuffed animals is, of course, Christopher Robin.

I realize that while I may have made a few of you laugh at my analysis of Winnie the Pooh and company, I probably made more of you angry. How much lower can a person get than to take some of the most beloved, innocent characters in children's literature (and cartoons for that matter), and completely ruin their image? Yet that is exactly what we do to each other on a daily basis. We pass judgment on others by what we see, and too often, we are looking for what is wrong with a person instead of what is right. Abraham Lincoln once said, "Those who look for the bad in people will surely find it."[1]

God is an artist, and his favorite media is clay. The prophet Isaiah said, "But now, O Lord, You are our Father, We are the clay, and You our potter; And all of us are the work of Your hand."[2] He molds and forms us into the vessels that He wants. It must break His heart when we mock or deride others for what we perceive as physical deficiencies, intellectual shortcomings, emotional imbalances, or personality disorders. Take your pick. We write people off without giving them a second chance because they don't meet our standards of perfection. Well, I've got a news flash for you: everyone has *something* wrong with them, and some of us have more things wrong with us than others do. To impugn the art is to impugn the artist. When we show contempt for others, we show contempt for God and the great value they have in His eyes. They are His creation made in His image. Rather sobering, isn't it?

Sadly enough, the things we so gladly point out as defective in others are often things they cannot change. And it's all for the sake of making ourselves feel more important or special, based on the attitude, "Thank God I'm not like them." Whether we say it to their faces or not, the damage to those people is real.

We deride the image of God in them as human beings, and they could not be more maligned.

I can't tell you how many people I have come across who want nothing to do with Christianity because of the way they see us treating each other. Yet didn't Jesus say, "By this all men will know that you are My disciples, if you have love for one another"?[3] If we treat each other meanly, then how will we treat those who are outside the family of God?

To any of those who may be reading this and are not yet followers of Jesus, I want to apologize for the lack of true Christ-like love that has been demonstrated and shared with you. I also want to apologize to those in the body of Christ who have been discounted, ignored, or relegated to second class by those who are "better." Few things in life really make me want to put the holy smack down on someone more than when I see people being treated like trash—like they don't matter—especially by the self-righteous and pious who think their mere presence is a blessing to the more unfortunate around them.

The Bible defines real love in several places, but the most comprehensive picture is found in I Corinthians 13, the Love Chapter. The passage opens by saying that you can be the most spiritual, supernatural, and giving person on the planet, but if you do not have love, you are a total zero. It goes on to specifically outline what love looks like, feels like, and acts like. I'd like to end this chapter with a portion of that passage. Let the Holy Spirit examine you in light of this scripture and point out those times, places, and ways where you have fallen short. Then, let Him define you as you commit to becoming the living embodiment of the Word . . . the embodiment of God's love to a world in desperate need of it.

"If I speak in the tongues of men and angels, but have not love, I am only a resounding gong or a clanging cymbal. If I have the gift of prophecy and can fathom all mysteries and all knowledge, and if I have a faith that can move mountains, but have not love, I am nothing. If I give all I possess to the poor and surrender my body to the flames, but have not love, I gain nothing.

"Love is patient, love is kind. It does not envy, it does not boast, it is not proud. It is not rude, it is not self-seeking, it is not easily angered, it keeps no record of wrongs. Love does not delight in evil but rejoices with the truth. It always protects, always trusts, always hopes, always perseveres. Love never fails.[4]"

## Think About It

- When were you picked on for your imperfections?
- How did that make you feel?
- When have you picked on others for their imperfections or for being different?
- How did that make you feel?
- Did you notice any reaction in that person, whether immediate or later?
- What do you do when you see someone being harassed?
- When was the last time you deliberately reached out to the outcast?
- Was there a time when you came to someone's rescue?
- How did that make you feel?
- Take some time this week to think about those people who "bother" you the most or that you see get picked on a lot; then, find the good things in them, and tell them what you see.

# CHAPTER TWELVE

# Stupid Desires

# or

# Be Careful What You Wish

# for . . .

Some things are by invitation only. Brandings are like that. I pastored a church in Spray, Oregon for several years, and every year during early spring, all the ranchers would prepare their cattle for "release"— during the winter, the herds are kept in pens so they can't wander up in the mountains and get caught in a sudden storm. So with the coming of spring, the ranchers "work" and then release the herd. *Working a herd* means sorting, inoculating, branding, tagging, and turning bull calves into steers. The people work hard, but they also have fun. The host rancher always provides a great meal when everyone finishes. Let me tell you, the meal is the highlight—a mini Thanksgiving of sorts.

But as I said, brandings are by invitation only. A person doesn't just show up to one expecting to work and eat. An invitation to a branding is an honor. I was in Spray for two years before my family and I got our first invitation, and I was psyched. I knew this friendly, albeit somewhat guarded community, was accepting me and since I was the only pastor in this town of 150 people, this was a huge breakthrough.

Although I had spent my childhood summers on my aunt and uncle's dairy farm, the ranching experience was something totally different. A definite greenhorn, I had no qualms about my role: do what they tell me to do. I did a lot of grunt work, and I did not complain. They had finally invited me to a branding, and this was something I'd always wanted.

Part of the grunt work included climbing inside the pens to help sort the calves from the mature animals. We opened and closed various gates in order to get the cattle to the right place for each step in the process; however, we were not just working with calves, like in chapter ten. We were working with cows, too.

All animals are not the same, and as comical as it may seem, some of those cows had a real attitude problem. They gave el Diablo a run for his money. Not only obstinate, a couple of these cows were just downright mean and dangerous. In the midst of all our yelling, waving, and pushing, one of the fences was knocked loose. Made of tubular metal, this fence stood eight feet high, affixed directly to a sheer rock wall. The gate to the pen we were in happened to attach to this piece of fence, so we had to stop the work.

I began helping Eddie, the rancher's son, repair the fence while some of the other workers kept the cows at the other end of the pen. Before I go any further, let me describe to you my stature: I am 5 feet 9 inches tall and all of 140 pounds. Eddie, on the other hand, has me beat on height and weight; he weighs over 200 pounds. Eddie stood next to the fence and the rock's face, tightening up the bolts, while I stood next to him, doing whatever he told me to do.

Most people prefer being the ones who yell "Look out!" rather than being the one yelled at. When you hear it shouted several times, you know you're in trouble. Apparently, one of those cows with attitude didn't like the workers holding her up at the other end of the corral and made a break for it. After the fourth "Look out!" I turned to see what all the fuss was about: this full-grown 2,000-pound angry cow was running at top speed and headed straight for me. Nearly face-to-face, I could have reached out and poked it in the eye *with my elbow.* I did mention that I only weigh 140 pounds, right? The cow was going to run me straight into Eddie, the rock wall, and the fence.

I didn't pray. I didn't shout. There was no time. I simply thought, *I'm dead.* I believed I was about to die. I was going to be killed by a cow. How do you explain that kind of thing to God? God has a reputation for asking rhetorical questions. He asked Adam and Eve, "Where are you?" when they were hiding. He asked Moses, "What is that in your hand?" when he was holding a staff. God asked Elijah twice, "What are you doing here, Elijah?" when he was hiding on a mountain from a murderous queen. Did He not already know?

DUH! I could not imagine having to face the same kind of questions.

"What are you doing here, John?"

"I am in the right place, aren't I?"

"Yes, you are in the right place, but you are a bit early. So, what are you doing here?"

"I died."

"Yes, and how . . . ?"

"Well, I got hit by a cow."

"You got hit by a cow?"

Would He know all of this? Of course He would. But having to explain it all, and not only to Him, but to all of your friends and family FOR ETERNITY!? How do you live something down when you are dealing with eternity? I would forever be known as the guy who died because he was run over by a cow!

And then it happened. It was an absolute miracle of God. With nowhere else to go and running at a full sprint, the cow jumped. Not just any jump, but an Olympic, world-class jump. That cow leapt clean over all 5 feet and 9 inches of me. I watched that animal soar from head to hooves, from udder to tail. It *flew* over me. And not only me but over Eddie, too. By now you must be thinking, "Where did it go?"

That fat cow managed to clear not only both Eddie and me, but it proceeded to go *through* the fence we were trying to fix. I can still see and hear that cow with tremendous banging, kicking, and clanging as it squeezed itself through the three-foot gap between the top two rungs of the fence, which were five feet off the ground. And it did all of that without knocking the gate over to boot! Either that was a Supercow or a mutant X-Cow. Considering I didn't see an "S" on that cow's chest from my special vantage point, I'm leaning towards the X-cow theory.

First, I felt pure shock. I could not believe what I had just been a party to. All that, and no one had videotaped the event for my $10,000 reward from America's Funniest Home Videos. That idea quickly vanished and rage took its place (remember, don't lose your temper!). The knuckleheads at the other end of the pen didn't do their job, and I almost paid for it with my life. The rage subsided as quickly as the shock. I next felt that I *really* did not want to be there anymore. I wanted to go home. This feeling stayed with me. But what could I do? It took over two years to get an invitation. I had wanted this. If I left now, I could guarantee that by nightfall the entire town would have heard, "Pastor John bailed." They would never ask me to attend another branding again. There was nothing left to do but go back to work.

Allow me to draw a correlation between a relationship with God and the experience of my first branding. Attending a branding was something that I desperately wanted, but when it finally came, it wasn't exactly what I expected. Not only that, I was left with the conflicting proposition of staying or leaving. The people of Israel faced just such an occurrence.

For four hundred years, the Israelites lived in the land of Egypt, and for the vast majority of that time, they spent it as slaves under Pharaoh and the Egyptians. After centuries of crying out to God, He finally delivered them from bondage. Even as the Lord was setting them free through Moses and the ten plagues, they questioned whether or not it was worth it to be set free[1] because Pharaoh made things exponentially more difficult for them. Once the tenth plague hit, Pharaoh kicked them out of the country, although he changed his mind and tried to re-enslave them. But God miraculously delivered them through the parting of the Red Sea. As awesome as that was, the best lay ahead.

Set free from slavery, the Hebrews began their journey to the land God promised them through their forefather, Abraham. Along the way, they learned many important things, especially the proper way to worship God and what he expected of them as a people in terms of morals and laws. The Hebrews differed from the surrounding nations—their worship of the one true God and their adherence to His commands marked them as "set apart." Of course, we know the "short list" of these edicts as the Ten Commandments. God gave quite a few more laws to the Israelites, but these ten stand out as a central code of ethics. Interesting to note is the way they received the laws.

God told Moses to have the people prepare themselves for His visitation.[2] They did so through a three-day consecration period in anticipation of the Lord's descending upon Mt. Sinai, the mountain where they were encamped. Earlier, when they had called upon the Lord for deliverance, He delivered them with never-before-seen miraculous demonstrations. Now, God was about to speak to the people *directly*: "So it came about on the third day, when it was morning, that there were thunder and lightning flashes and a thick cloud upon the mountain and a very loud trumpet sound, so that all the people who were in the camp trembled. And Moses brought the people out of the camp to meet God, and they stood at the foot of the mountain. Now Mount Sinai was all in smoke because the Lord descended upon it in fire; and its smoke ascended like the smoke of a furnace, and the whole mountain quaked violently."[3]

God sends Moses down the mountain to warn the people not to try to climb the mountain: "So Moses went down to the people and told them. Then God spoke all these words saying, 'I am the Lord your God, who brought you out of the land of Egypt, out of the house of slavery.'"[4] At this point, God is speaking to the entire assembly of the Israelites. As the passage moves forward, we see that He gave all of the Ten Commandments to the Hebrews orally before he gave Moses the inscribed version on the famous stone tablets. Just in case we forget the gravity of the situation, the text gives us a vivid reminder of what is happening:

"All the people perceived the thunder and the lightning flashes and the sound of the trumpet and the mountain smoking; and when the people saw it, they trembled and stood at a distance. Then they said to

Moses, 'Speak to us yourself and we will listen; but let not God speak to us or we will die.' Moses said to the people, 'Do not be afraid; for God has come in order to test you, and in order that the fear of Him may remain with you, so that you may not sin.' So the people stood at a distance, while Moses approached the thick cloud where God was.[5]

They saw the manifest presence of God on the mountain! God *spoke* to these people! Is this not what they wanted? They called on the Lord when they were in bondage, and He showed up. Up to this point in the journey, all they did was complain about Him, and now they have the chance to see and hear from Him personally. Yet instead of embracing God, they decide that they've had enough of Him: "Moses, you go talk to Him; we'll stay right here." Was the experience awesome and hair-raising? Of course it was. IT WAS GOD! But even as we have read, Moses tried to encourage them to not be afraid. Still, they wanted to meet God on their own terms, not on His.

Here is the scary part of the story. Moses spends quite a bit of time on Mt. Sinai with God—forty days and nights, in fact.[6] In the meantime, the people gather around Aaron and say, "Come, make us a god who will go before us; as for this Moses, the man who brought us up from the land of Egypt, we do not know what has become of him."[7] Excuse me? You are still in the shadow of a mountain that is burning, smoking, and shaking because of the presence of GOD, and you are going to ask the second in command, the future high priest, to make an idol to take HIS place? And wonder of wonders, Aaron does it! When he finishes fashioning this idol, his declaration rings familiar: "This is your god, O Israel, who brought you up out of the land of Egypt."[8] That was the first thing the *real* God said to the people before He gave them the Big Ten. Now they credited God's acts to a statue of gold. If not for the intercession of Moses, the Lord would have wiped out the lot of them and started fresh with Moses.

The Hebrews had what they wanted—had what they asked for—and when it became too much, they changed their minds and cashed in a genuine relationship with God for a statue of a calf. I find it stupefying that when we ask for God to show up, and He does, all of a sudden, we don't want Him anymore because He's too much to handle. It needs to be said that a relationship with God will always be more than what we expect and more than we can handle. HE IS GOD!

The disciples experienced the same thing when they saw Jesus feed the five thousand and walk on water.[9] Right after those miracles, Jesus started dispensing some really hard things to accept. A good number of his followers decided that it was all too much and left. Turning to the twelve disciples, Jesus asks them if they are going to leave, too. Peter replied, "Lord, to whom shall we go? You have the words of eternal life."[10] Unlike his forefathers, Peter knew that as unnerving and unsettling as walking with the Lord can be, the only real option is to remain with Him.

## Think About It

- When have you asked God to show up or help you?

- Were your encounters with God what you expected? How were they different?

- Have you had a "scary" moment with the Lord? What happened?

- At this point, have you chosen to embrace God or push Him away?

# CHAPTER THIRTEEN

# Stupid Ministry
# or
# I Did Not Sign Up For This

I had always felt called to the senior pastorate, but as everyone in ministry knows, you always start out working with children and youth first. After a twelve-year winding road with enough ups and downs to make a sailor seasick, I finally felt settled after a few months of pastoring in Spray, Oregon. Life was wonderful!!!

I came into the church a year after their last pastor had left, so I quickly established a "game plan" to help the congregation move forward. For one thing, a thriving group of teenagers lived in this town of 150 people, and I didn't want them getting bored and doing something silly, like, I don't know, shooting cars with BB guns.

During this time, my wife and I became friends with a young couple, Destry and Cami Brown, who loved God and teenagers. We needed leaders for the youth group, and they fit the bill. They were energetic, industrious, fun, committed to the Lord, hungry to learn, and passionate for kids. More importantly, we knew they were God's choice for this vital ministry. I just needed to convince them of that.

Spray is a ranching community, and the Browns are cowboy through and through. Destry managed one of the larger local ranches *and* ran his own herd. After church one Sunday morning, I asked him about meeting that week. He replied, "I'm missing a cow and need to go find her. If I do find her, we can meet tomorrow. Will that work?" Of course it would work. Based on our previous chats, I knew asking him and his wife to lead the youth ministry would be a simple and straight-forward matter.

The next morning, Destry called: "I couldn't find that cow. If you still want to meet, come out to the ranch, and we can talk and look for the cow at the same time." I would not be caught unprepared for this visit. On another occasion, I went to see one of my ranching congregants in order to pray for him. After the prayer, he asked if I would help him move his herd: "It won't take long," he'd assured me. OK, why not? I ended up hornswoggled into helping him move his herd OVER A MOUNTAIN all the while dressed in some fairly nice clothes and shoes—and it took *all* day. I would not let that kind of thing happen again. So when I met with Destry, I felt appropriately dressed in jeans, a casual collared shirt, and sneakers. Boy was I wrong. I needed a hazmat suit.

Destry asked me to climb into his truck. As we rode along, he began explaining his concern for this particular cow: "This cow is pregnant and should've calved by now. I can't find her or her calf. She might be in distress, and if so, we'll have to help her." I thought, *We're going to calve. No big deal. I helped deliver calves every summer on my uncle's dairy farm. This will be just like old times.* But first we had to find her, and she'd been missing for three days. Known for its coyotes, Spray also witnesses an occasional bear and cougar—we hoped to find the missing cow and calf before they became a meal.

We drove down one of the dirt roads, heading towards the back fields of the ranch. At this point, I decided to jump right into my presentation: we needed youth leaders, and I believed the Lord wanted Destry and Cami to fill these roles. We talked about the vision, purpose, and direction of the ministry. Our conversation didn't even last five minutes. Both he and Cami "felt" this was the purpose for my visit and had previously decided that if I offered the position, they would take it. HA HA! This was too easy. Excitement ran through me. I could see everything coming together. Pastoring this place was going to be a blast. We traveled on and talked another ten minutes or so, and then, he spotted her.

The cow lay in the grass a good twenty yards off the road under a tree. At first, she looked dead. However, when we pulled off the road, she lifted her head slightly. I saw the concern on Destry's face. Stepping out of the truck, I quickly understood the gravity of the situation as I breathed in an unbelievable stench. We smelled her from fifteen yards away, and it grew more eye watering and nose burning with every step we took. I quickly pulled my shirt over my nose.

Then the flies caught my attention. Being poop machines, cattle come with flies, they naturally draw insects. But this landed in the "plague of Egypt" category. In all my life, I have never seen so many flies in one place. Their noise alone nearly drove me crazy. The zillion noisy flies also apparently suffered from ADHD: they covered us, crawling into our eyes, ears, and hair . . . it's a good thing my shirt covered my mouth. Opening one's mouth invited a second breakfast.

When we got to her, we found a pair of small hooves poking out of the cow's womb. Destry began to diagnose the situation and point certain things out to me. I really didn't want to know, but I guess since the cow was lying in an enormous puddle of goo, he felt compelled to explain. The calf was dead and the cow had been trying to pass it for some time, possibly for days. That calf had to come out and fast.

Stillbirths are very hard on a cow. A live calf actually helps in the birthing process. When the contractions come, the calf will tense up. Both calf and cow push against each other, making things move along quickly. Without that tension, the cow had been laboring endlessly with little to show for it.

Destry ran back to his truck and came back with a winch and a box of gloves. While he affixed the winch to the tree, he explained, "This calf will only come out if we pull it out. But before I attach this end to the hooves, I have to straighten the calf out."

He pulled a pair of gloves out of the box. I expected to see some nice rubber surgical-type gloves. Instead, he pulled out flimsy, plastic cafeteria gloves—the one-size-fits-all kind where you can't tell which digit represents the thumb versus the pinky. He donned a pair and set to doing what needed to be done—he put his hands *inside* the cow's womb and began to reposition the calf. That's when I thought, *Yeah buddy, that's why you da Ranchah, and I'm da Pastah! Ha ha! Have fun with that!*

He wasn't having any fun and neither was the cow. She began to struggle against him and kick her legs, so Destry told me to hold the cow's head down and make sure she didn't stand up. Once he got the calf positioned properly, he pulled his hands out and the cow settled down again. Destry quickly wrapped the cable around the hooves and took up the slack. The winch creaked and clacked as Destry worked the lever. Slowly the calf began to come out. Obviously this caused the cow more distress, but at least this time, she didn't try to stand up. Now nature began to take hold, and it appeared that the cow was actually working with Destry.

First we saw ankles, shins, and knees, and then we started to see the head. The face was out now up to the crown of its head, and that's when I saw the most gruesome scene I have ever witnessed. The skin was peeling off the skull around the lips, the tongue was hanging out of its mouth, and the eyes were glazed and half rolled back in its head. We were discovering a whole new level of putrefaction.

At that moment, the winch broke. With a grinding crack, something gave way, and it ceased working altogether. We looked at each other in disbelief.

I tried not to laugh as I said, "Destry, this just isn't your day."

He picked up the box of gloves and tossed it to me, also trying not to laugh. "I'm not the only one who's going to have a bad day."

I really did not like the sound of that.

We had no way of pulling the calf out on our own without the winch. Our only option pointed to repairing the winch, which meant unhooking it and taking it to the ranch shop. And of course, Destry had to do this. He gave me a special assignment: I had to hold the dead calf and keep it from moving. If the calf slid back into the cow, our situation would only get worse. The calf might very well go all the way back in, and if that happened . . . well, that wasn't going to happen if Destry could help it. Then he said, "You're going to want to put a pair of those on."

Woohoo! Thanks for the news flash, Captain Obvious. I sat down behind the cow and made sure my shirt was firmly in place over my nose. While I was putting on my "protection," Destry told me I needed to grab the legs up by the knees so he would have room to unhook the cable. This was going to be gross. I gripped the dead calf, and Destry removed the winch. I could feel the pull, so I squeezed the slimy legs a little firmer.

Destry gathered his equipment and headed for the truck, saying he'd return as soon as he could. As he climbed in the cab, he shouted, "Don't let her get up!" I'm seated on the ground behind a cow with my shirt on my face and my nose in my armpit, trying to live on my deodorant. I have two handfuls of rotting, juicy calf carcass. The number of flies buzzing around me could short out an industrial bug zapper. On top of all of this, Destry wants to make sure I don't let the cow get up. *Right.*

I started doing the math in my head. *It took us about fifteen minutes to get out here, but then again, we drove slowly, looking for this wretched animal. If Destry steps on it, he could get to the shop and back with a total travel time of ten minutes. Hopefully, the winch won't take more than ten minutes to fix. So I might be here for around twenty minutes.* Since I had nothing better to do, I began to count to sixty . . . twenty times.

Every now and then the cow would move, probably because of a contraction. My rear end started hurting, my legs began cramping, and my fingers felt a little stiff, but I was up to sixty for the tenth time. If this really marked the halfway point, I wasn't concerned, even with my current level of discomfort.

I had nearly reached sixty for the twentieth time when I felt the calf begin to slip back into the cow. I could *not* let that happen, so I bore down and squeezed those little legs as hard as possible. It didn't help. In fact, it seemed worse. Suddenly, the cow gave a lurch. Half startled, I snapped my head up to see what happened and when I did, my shirt came off of my face.

The hide had torn just above both knees and was bunching up in my fingers like the paper wrapper on a straw as the legs slid through my hands. That was why I was losing the calf. First with my right and then with my left, I let go of each leg and reached up to get ahold of the knees again. Only now instead of skin, I was gripping the ivory white of exposed bone. The sight and unhindered smell of it all was almost too much. At this moment, I realized that the flies, which were landing and feasting on the calf, were crawling all over me. I retched. The last thing I needed was to throw up. I calmed myself by thinking that at any minute now, I would hear the sound of Destry's truck coming up the road to my rescue. Any minute now. Yup. He'll be pulling up at any moment . . .

Little did I know that the winch was broken beyond repair. Destry traveled into town in order to borrow one. His foray would take nearly an hour, but I didn't know that. The minutes kept slipping by and after a while, I quit counting. About forty minutes ticked away, and by this time, I *really* hurt. Destry and I had finished our conversation. Now the Lord and I were going to have one.

"I did not sign up for this. This is not ministry."

When I got a reply of, "Oh, really?" I knew I was about to learn something.

Just what does it mean to be in ministry? This question applies to every Christian because we are all called to ministry, not only pastors. According to Paul, Jesus set pastors in churches "for the equipping of the saints for the work of service, to the building up of the body of Christ."[1] The job of ministers involves preparing the people under their care to do the greater work of the ministry. However, too often, clergy are installed into a church or parish with the people thinking, *Well, get to work and minister to us and this community.* All the while, however, the clergy's perspective looks like this: "Ok, I'm going to give you the tools, knowledge, and support you need in order to minister."

What does ministry look like? It looks like a wrestling match with death, and it deals with the worst things people have inside of them. I can't tell you how many times I've seen "saintly" people get upset when "sinners" come into the church and start "messing things up." It would be comedic if it were not so tragic. For starters, where are they supposed to go? The church is supposed to be the place of hope, change, possibility, and renewal. Do we expect the lost to get found on their own? I contend that if there aren't any sinners in our churches, then our churches really aren't churches. They're Christian social clubs.

Jesus constantly made the religious people angry because He hung out with the dregs of society. St. Mark recounts an occasion when Jesus explained himself to the Pharisees: "It is not those that are healthy who need a physician, but those who are sick; I did not come to call the righteous, but sinners."[2] When Luke tells the parable of The Lost Sheep, he notes that Jesus said He would leave ninety-nine sheep to go find the one lost.[3] If you can't find or feel Jesus in your church, it may be because there are no sinners in it. He has left you to go out in the community in order to find the lost ones.

Then there is the assumption that because we are Christians, we are okay. If we are honest with ourselves, we KNOW this is not true. Just because we are believers doesn't mean we don't struggle with sin and temptation. We just know how to put up a false front so the other "saints" don't see it. Thank God for the apostle Paul who was willing to let us see his own struggles.[4] If we call anyone a saint, I think we'd all agree it would be Paul. His contributions to the Word of

God, his missionary journeys, and the countless persecutions he suffered place him in a class by himself.

Paul deals with the duality all Christians face, including himself—the battle between our own flesh and its desires and the Spirit and what He desires. Paul said, "I know that nothing good lives in me, that is, in my sinful nature. For I have the desire to do what is good, but I cannot carry it out. For what I do is not the good I want to do; no, the evil I do not want to do—this I keep on doing."[5]

Paul called out for help and found the answer: "What a wretched man I am! Who will rescue me free from this body of death? Thanks be to God—through Jesus Christ our Lord!"[6] The answer for sinner and saint alike is Jesus. He alone can deliver us from our sins, ourselves, and death.

So what is ministry? It is holding on to someone else's death until Jesus comes and delivers. I could not deliver that calf—only Destry could. My job was to hold onto it. We cannot deliver ourselves or others from sin. Only Jesus can. We are called to minister to them by holding on with them until that delivery happens. Is it gross? Yes. Is it ugly? Yes. Wearisome? Tiring? Painful? Yes, yes, yes. But in the end, it brings life. The next year, that cow gave birth to a live calf. Destry was grateful for my help, and if the cow could talk, I know it would express its gratitude as well. How much more would those whose death you have embraced express their gratitude for helping them find life? How much more would Jesus?

## Think About It

- Is your church open to sinners? For that matter, are you? To prostitutes, thieves, gangsters, and drug addicts?
- Who is being delivered through you and the ministry of your parish/congregation?
- When was the last time you embraced someone's death until Jesus delivered him or her?
- What price did you pay? What suffering did you endure to see someone delivered?
- What is the death inside of you? What are you struggling with?
- Are you hiding it, or are you allowing someone to minister to you until Jesus delivers you?

# CHAPTER FOURTEEN

## Stupid Kid
## or
## You Won't Get It Until You Got It

As a little boy, I loved trains. I wore a pair of blue-and-white striped engineer overalls all the time. I was wearing them when *it* happened. There I was: a little five-year-old kindergartener wearing a simple t-shirt, a pair of sneakers, and my favorite Oshkosh bib overalls.

My family and I attended Calvary United Methodist church in Waldorf, Maryland. That

November, our church held a series of nighttime services. My mother took Alan, Kathleen, and me to church, and I sat on the aisle end of the pew with my mom next to me, then Kathleen, and then Alan.

Of course, I don't remember everything the guest preacher said, but I remember a few things. I remember how he talked about God—that God is love and He loves everyone. If I wanted God's love, I could have it. I remember how he talked about Jesus—that God sent Jesus to die on the cross for my sins, and then He raised Jesus back to life. If I asked God to forgive me, He would take my sins away. I remember how the preacher talked about heaven—that Jesus was there now. If I loved God and received Jesus into my heart and life, then I could go to heaven someday and live with Jesus forever. I remember how he talked about God's plan for me—that God had a purpose for my whole life. If I lived for God, I would find joy and peace, even when things became hard.

At the end of his sermon, the preacher asked everyone to stand while he gave an invitation. Anyone who wanted God's love and forgiveness through Jesus could come forward and pray—anyone who wanted to go to heaven someday and have God in their life could come forward and pray.

"Come to the altar and give your life to Jesus," he said. "He will be with you forever."

What can the mind of a kindergartner grasp? I didn't know nor understand theological terms, like *justification*, *propitiation*, or *incarnation*. I'd never heard of Calvin or Arminius or the unending debates between their schools of thought and scriptural interpretation. I could not conceive denominational lines, such as Catholic, Baptist, Methodist, Reformed, Assemblies of God, Church of God in Christ, and Independent. For me, church was church. I couldn't even read my own mother tongue let alone Greek, Hebrew, or Aramaic.

All I knew was that what the man up front was saying sounded good to me. I wanted Jesus in my heart and life. I wanted to go to heaven someday. I wanted to be a good boy. Certainly a five year old hasn't racked up a pile of sins the way an older person might have, but I still knew some things I had done were bad. I wanted to be forgiven.

I already had one foot out in the aisle when I looked up at my mom and asked her, "Can I go?"

Everyone in the pew was obviously caught off guard because they looked at me as if I had two heads. But all I saw was a reassuring nod. I don't know if she said anything because I was out of earshot in a matter of seconds. There was only one place I wanted to be, and it was at the altar.

A few other adults came forward as well, but I was the only kid. When I got to the altar, our pastor, Rev. Culp, came straight to me, but he wasn't the only person there. As I knelt on the carpeted step of the communion rail, I bowed my head, folded my hands to pray, and felt the presence of God. From my current perspective, I could use a variety of words to describe what I felt as I prayed and gave my life to Jesus. As a little boy, however, I only had one word to explain what was going on inside of me: *good*. The goodness of God was filling me. His love and kindness were surrounding me. I was totally oblivious to everything else going on around me. It was Jesus, my pastor, and me—and it was *good*.

I may have only been a stupid kid, ignorant of the world and its ways, but I knew one thing for sure: I had been forgiven. As I stood up from the altar, I felt lighter. When I went back to the pew where my mother was, I started jumping up and down. I told her, "I feel light." I couldn't stop jumping. I knew I had been changed, that Jesus was in my heart, and I would be going to heaven.

The gospel of Jesus Christ is very simple. It's the kind of thing even a child can grasp. Actually, Jesus told His disciples, "Truly I say to you, unless you are converted and become like children, you will not enter the kingdom of heaven."[1] He said this to underscore the simple childlike faith that one must express in order to begin a relationship with Him. However, as simple as the gospel is, you won't get it until you got it.

It all starts with God's love: "For God so loved the world, that He gave His only begotten Son, that whoever believes in Him shall not perish but have eternal life."[2] Even though we have offended the Lord, He still loves us.

In the book of Romans, Paul gives some excellent explanations that outline how salvation works. He starts out by telling us the plain truth about humankind: "For all have sinned and fall short of the glory of God."[3] There isn't anyone who hasn't sinned against God, big or small. What is the result of that sin? "For the wages of sin is death, but the free gift of God is eternal life in

Christ Jesus our Lord."[4] We deserve death (hell), but God wants to give us life (heaven).

Again, God's love for us motivates His desire to give us life: "But God demonstrates his own love for us in this: while we were still sinners, Christ died for us."[5] We don't have to try to get our act together and then come to God. That's impossible. Nothing we do will absolve our sins before Him. That is why the Father sent Jesus to make a way for us so we can have eternal life with Him.

Jesus accomplished this through His death and resurrection: "He was delivered over to death for our sins and was raised to life for our justification."[6] Jesus, the Son of God, died on the cross, bearing all of our sins. Three days later, He was raised to life again as proof that His sacrifice was acceptable. For that reason, we can ask for and find forgiveness from God because of Jesus.

How is this done? Paul shares the simple, straightforward steps for starting a new life with God: "If you confess with your mouth, Jesus as Lord, and believe in your heart that God raised Him from the dead, you will be saved; for with the heart a person believes, resulting in righteousness, and with the mouth he confesses, resulting in salvation. For the Scripture says, 'Whoever believes in Him will not be disappointed.' For there is no distinction between Jew and Greek; for the same Lord is Lord of all, abounding in riches for all who call on Him; for 'Whoever calls on the name of the Lord will be saved.'[7]

Just believe. Believe that God loves you. Believe that Jesus died for you. Believe that He was raised from the dead for you. Believe that He wants to forgive you, and all you need to do is ask. Confess your sins, ask God to forgive you, and ask Him into your life. Really difficult, isn't it?

All these years later, I can look back on that day and know the truth of the promise when Jesus said, "I will never leave you nor forsake you." Have I made mistakes? Have I sinned since then? Of course I have. Even as a pastor and minister trying to lead others in a relationship with Christ, I have had my moments of failure. Some of the things you have read are evidence enough of that. Through it all, I have known the great forgiveness of God. When I need it, I go back to that little boy. A five-year-old kindergartener could, and does, believe. What can you believe?

## Think About It

- Have you ever asked God to forgive you?
- What is keeping you from accepting God's gift of eternal life?
- Do you need to go back to the beginning and renew your faith?
- What is your testimony? When and how did you meet Jesus?

The following prayer will help you if you want to begin or renew your walk with God. It's very simple. Confess and repent of your sins. Then, accept God's forgiveness, and let Him come into your life:

God, I know that I have sinned against You, and I'm sorry. I believe that You love me and sent Jesus to die for me. I also believe that He was raised from the dead so I could be forgiven. Right now I ask You to forgive me. I accept and thank You for Your forgiveness. I want to live for You and ask that You come into my life. In Jesus' name, amen.

If you prayed this prayer, I want you to tell someone who you know is a Christian. If you attend church and have a pastor, I encourage you to tell your pastor as well. If you don't have a church, I encourage you to find a good, Bible-believing one with a minister that will love you and help you grow in your life with the Lord.

## About the Author

Rev. John P. King, M.A., is an ordained Assembly of God minister. He graduated from Valley Forge Christian College in 1990 with a bachelor's degree in Bible with a concentration in Pastoral Studies. From there, he worked as a children and youth pastor for 8 years and a senior pastor for 8 years. He is presently employed as a performance coach and prayer team supervisor at CBN's Prayer Center in Virginia Beach and also contributes to CBN.com's daily devotions as a staff writer. In May of 2012 he completed his M.A. in Practical Theology from Regent University. John and his wife, Genevieve, have been married for 22 years and have two grown children, Kenneth and Emily.

# ENDNOTES

## Chapter One

[1]Proverbs 22:24-25 (NIV)

[2]I Corinthians 15:33 (NASB)

[3]Proverbs 13:20 (NASB)

## Chapter Two

[1]II Samuel 11:1-27

[2]II Samuel 21:15-17

[3]II Samuel 21:17b(NASB)

[4]Jeremiah 29:11 (NIV)

[5]Ephesians 2:10 (NASB)

[6]http://www.goodreads.com/author/quotes/44567 Theodore_Roosevelt

## Chapter Three

[1]Galatians 6:6-9 (NASB)

[2]Hebrews 12:5-6 (NIV)

[3]Hebrews 12:10-11 (NIV)

[4]Deuteronomy 28

[5]Deuteronomy 30:19-20 (NASB)

---

## Chapter Four

[1]Luke 15:11-32

[2]*The American Heritage Dictionary,* Second College Edition, s.v. "prodigal."

[3]Luke 15:21 (NASB)

[4]Luke 15:32 (NASB)

[5] Luke 15:31-32a (NASB)

[6]Romans 2:1-11

[7]Romans 2:4 (NASB)

[8]II Peter 3:9

## Chapter Five

[1]Proverbs 3:12 (NASB)

[2]Jeremiah 2:1-3 (NIV)

[3]Numbers 14

[4]Deuteronomy 29:5

## Chapter Six

[1]The federal government cannot account for $24.5 billion spent in 2003. Examples of Government Waste published on September 14, 2005, by Brian Riedl: http://www.heritage.org/research/reports/2005/09/examples-of-government-waste

---

[2] "The Decade in Pork: Ten Years of Ear Mark Spending," by Robert Longley, *About.com*, http://usgovinfo.about.com/od/federalbudgetprocess/a/porkdecade.htm

[3] Matthew 28:18-20 (NASB)

[4] Mark 16:15-18 (NASB)

[5] Matthew 25:14-30

## Chapter Seven

*Name changed out of respect for the families.
[1] John 21:18-24

## Chapter Eight

[1] I Samuel 27

[2] I Samuel 29

[3] I Samuel 30:3 (NASB)

[4] I Samuel 30:6 (NASB)

[5] I Samuel 30

## Chapter Nine

[1] Proverbs 16:18 (NASB)

[2] Proverbs 3:34, James 4:6, and I Peter 5:5

[3]Luke 22:24-27 (NASB)

## Chapter Ten

[1]Numbers 12:1-16 (NASB)

[2]Exodus 33:11 (NASB)

[3]Exodus 2:11-14

[4]Exodus 2:12 (NASB)

[5]Exodus 17:1-7

[6]Numbers 20:1-13

[7]Numbers 20:10 (NASB)

[8]Numbers 20:12 (NASB)

[9]Deuteronomy 3:23-27

[10]Deuteronomy 3:26 (NASB)

[11]James 1:19-20 (NASB)

## Chapter Eleven

[1]http://www.goodreads.com/author/quotes/229.Ab raham_Lincoln

[2]Isaiah 64:8 (NASB)

[3]John 13:35 (NASB)

[4]I Corinthians 13:1-8 (NIV)

## Chapter Twelve

[1]Exodus 5:15-23

[2]Exodus 19

[3]Exodus 19:16-18 (NASB)

[4]Exodus 19:25-20:2 (NASB)

[5]Exodus 20:18-20 (NASB)

[6]Exodus 24:18

[7]Exodus 32:1 (NASB)

[8]Exodus 32:4 (NASB)

[9]John 6

[10]John 6:68 (NASB)

## Chapter Thirteen

[1]Ephesians 4:11-12 (NASB)

[2]Mark 2:17 (NASB)

[3]Luke 15:1-7

[4]Romans 7:14-8:11

[5]Romans 7:18-19 (NIV)

[6]Romans 7:24 (NIV)

## Chapter Fourteen

[1]Matthew 18:3 (NASB)

[2]John 3:16 (NASB)

[3]Romans 3:23 (NASB)

[4]Romans 6:23 (NASB)

[5]Romans 5:8 (NIV)

[6]Romans 4:25 (NIV)

[7]Romans 10:9-13 (NASB)

Made in USA - Crawfordsville, IN
69078_9780615662954
10.28.2021 1819